ROUTLEDGE LIBRARY EDITIONS: CHINA UNDER MAO

Volume 10

MAO'S PREY

MAO'S PREY

The History of Chen Renbing,
Liberal Intelletual

JEANNETTE F. FORD

Routledge
Taylor & Francis Group

LONDON AND NEW YORK

First published in 2001 by Garland Publishing, Inc.

This edition first published in 2019
by Routledge
2 Park Square, Milton Park, Abingdon, Oxon OX14 4RN

and by Routledge
711 Third Avenue, New York, NY 10017

Routledge is an imprint of the Taylor & Francis Group, an informa business

British Library Cataloguing in Publication Data
A catalogue record for this book is available from the British Library

ISBN: 978-1-138-32344-5 (Set)
ISBN: 978-0-429-43659-8 (Set) (ebk)
ISBN: 978-1-138-34861-5 (Volume 10) (hbk)
ISBN: 978-1-138-34864-6 (Volume 10) (pbk)
ISBN: 978-0-429-43660-4 (Volume 10) (ebk)

Publisher's Note
The publisher has gone to great lengths to ensure the quality of this reprint but
points out that some imperfections in the original copies may be apparent.

Disclaimer
The publisher has made every effort to trace copyright holders and would welcome
correspondence from those they have been unable to trace.

MAO'S PREY
THE HISTORY OF CHEN RENBING, LIBERAL INTELLECTUAL

JEANNETTE FORD FERNANDEZ

Routledge
Taylor & Francis Group
LONDON AND NEW YORK

Published in 2001 by
Garland Publishing, Inc.
A member of the Taylor & Francis Group
711 Third Avenue
New York, NY 10017

2 Park Square, Milton Park
Abingdon, Oxfordshire
OX14 4RN

First issued in paperback 2014

Routledge is an imprint of the Taylor & Francis Group, an informa business

Library of Congress Cataloging-in-Publication Data is available from the Library of Congress.

ISBN 978-0-815-33949-6 (hbk)
ISBN 978-1-138-00186-2 (pbk)

Table of Contents

Preface

There is always more to be done. The purpose and scope of *Mao's Prey: The History of Chen Renbing, Liberal Intellectual* invites further research into the fate of modern Chinese intellectuals. This preliminary work, mitigated by the foibles of an outsider looking in, would not have been possible without a strong belief in the sincerity of individual efforts by Chinese intellectuals and indignation at their imposed limitations. Oral history plays an important part of *Mao's Prey* and makes it possible to confirm, as well as to explain, the professional and private lives of post-1949 intellectuals through the focal point of Chen Renbing, a man personally criticized by Mao Zedong.

Mao's Prey is the culmination of a tenacious and protracted pursuit. Chen Renbing (1909-1990) created the spark that led me to many years of research. He was forthright and brave to tell his story to a foreigner at a time in modern Chinese history when frankness was punishable and had long lost out to reticence.

How did the People's Republic of China inspire citizens in "grass-roots" mass mobilization campaigns after 1949? Mao Zedong's fledgling government appeared to have eliminated corruption, prostitution and drug addiction, enacted land reform, repudiated counter-revolutionary elements, reorganized the entire educational system and reeducated citizens to accept socialist ideology. These amazing changes were wrought in a few years and apparently with the enthusiastic backing of the citizenry in mass mobilization units. I wanted to learn more about how the Chinese leadership managed to engage citizens and in January 1979 I enrolled in the masters program in history at the State University of New York at Stony Brook.

My first visit to the People's Republic of China was in the summer of 1979 as a delegate with the US-China People's Friendship Association, a group that had promoted normalization of relations with China. I had studied Chinese at Nanyang University in Singapore a few years earlier in a senior year abroad program, and, my fascination with Chinese language and history that began at the State University of New York College at Brockport remained unabated.

One fateful morning in Shanghai during that 1979 summer, I didn't feel well and opted out of the morning excursion. I sat alone for a late breakfast musing on the view of the Bund from the 8th floor restaurant at the Peace Hotel. To my utter surprise I overheard a conversation in English at a nearby table where representatives from SUNY Stony Brook and Fudan University were discussing the forthcoming exchange program. I approached the group and took the first step towards continuing graduate studies at Fudan University. In August, 1980 I joined Shanghai's Fudan University History Department as the first exchange student from Stony Brook.

In China my topic, mass mobilization movements, was considered political science, a subject closed to foreigners. The foreign student officers at Fudan informed me that modern Chinese history was limited to events occurring before Mao Zedong proclaimed the People's Republic of China on October 1, 1949. I pondered about a substitute research question. Well, I reflected, I was a foreign student, and wouldn't it be interesting to understand what Chinese foreign students had achieved? The subject proved unwieldy because Chinese had studied in Japan, Europe, Russia and the United States and been involved in a broad range of political activities. I narrowed the topic to include those Chinese foreign students who went to the United States and returned to China within the time span I was allowed.

Approval was granted to design an oral history research project on Chinese intellectuals who had studied in the United States and returned to China from 1920-1950. I planned a longitudinal study of this group. What was their education and situation before going abroad, their experience in the United States, and their effect upon returning to China? I considered the richness of my thesis would be in highlighting the influences such American-returned intellectuals exerted in China. In retrospect my naiveté was astonishing.

School authorities introduced me to a few such intellectuals in Shanghai and Beijing and even accompanied me while I asked a set of sanctioned questions. After a time, I began to get informal information on individuals to interview. Usually the elderly intellectuals were eager to recall experiences before they went abroad and during their time in the United States. However, no one would talk about the period after 1949. I did not understand why until I met Dr. Chen Renbing.

I used to bicycle to his small apartment near the Shanghai sports stadium and film studio from my residence at the foreign student dormitory on the campus of Fudan University. Nearly every week for over a year, I pedaled across the city, armed with a small cassette recorder and notebook, wondering what exciting story would be told that day. Chen was extremely animated when he spoke and he would hasten to write some Chinese characters in my notebook to make sure I had the correct name of someone important to him or to clarify a historical point he was not sure I had grasped. He spoke to me almost exclusively in English and occasionally would even sing or play the piano when retelling some of his musical or theatrical experience.

When time came in the summer of 1982 for me to leave China I didn't know what to do with the explosive materials in my possession. Dr. Chen and I discussed the options. He gave me documents and photos to copy and I left him my manual typewriter and copies of my handwritten notes so that he could write his story. The manuscript came to me in bits and pieces, usually delivered by friends who carried it out of China and mailed it to me. His story, however, was only the start of my work. I set out to confirm what Dr. Chen told me and to widen the scope of information to see if his experience was characteristic of his peers. I researched the early study abroad phenomenon, the missionary enterprise, the policy of the Communist Party toward intellectuals, and tried to obtain primary source documents in order to fit together the web of information. I returned to China twice to gather materials and interview more intellectuals.

Dr. Chen wanted to see his story in print to honor his friends who met with disaster and imploringly asked about the publication prospects in our correspondence. Regrettably, my efforts were not enough to let him have his wish before he died in 1990. Perhaps he told the wrong person, perhaps another historian would have done a better job more rapidly. I find solace in supposing that hindsight and access to new research over the years provides more powerful insights than an earlier account might have accomplished.

This book is not his biography. Rather, *Mao's Prey* studies the life and times of a Chinese sociologist and how pivotal events in Chinese history influenced his perception of western learning and religion, and led to his political participation. Educated in the United States, (Ph.D. University of Michigan at Ann Arbor 1936), Chen embraced social responsibility in democratic movements from an early age. During the years before the twin struggles of civil war and Japanese invasion weighed heavily on the minds of all Chinese, Chen Renbing fancied himself a speech-maker and a voice of justice and democracy. Chen openly opposed the pre-1949 Nationalist government in writings and speeches and joined the China Democratic League, known as the "communist's little brother," as soon as the group decided to allow individual members.

After 1949, Chen embraced Mao's regime and was called upon to act as judge against alleged counter-revolutionaries in an open-air courtroom at the Shanghai racetrack. Chen Renbing was weaned on Dr. Sun Zhongshan's *Three Principles of the People* and western style democracy resulting from having come of age in a foreign mission enclave. He enjoyed his early post-

1949 positions of leadership and assumed that his opinions on matters of public policy were welcome, valued, and well-known. He was sadly mistaken.

Mao did not favor Chen's mixture of music, acting, and politics. Political devotion ruined Chen Renbing's first marriage even before the 1957 Anti-Rightist Campaign. His comments placed him in the select category of "Big Rightist." Thousands of intellectuals were targeted by Mao Zedong. The fragile communist party underestimated its control, particularly in light of how well intellectuals adapted to school reorganization in 1952. What if communists had not followed an anti-intellectual policy since the late 1920s? What if Mao Zedong had not subjugated intellectuals? Would Chinese have avoided the tragedy suffered by patriotic returned students and other intellectuals? Their ideological remolding began during the Thought Reform Movement. Subsequent mass mobilization campaigns were staged to further inculcate Marxist-Leninist-Mao Zedong Thought. Systematically, obstacles were placed in the path of a majority of intellectuals and prevented them from applying their learning and influence in China.

Special thanks are due to my professors in the United States. John Killigrew introduced me to Chinese history at the State University of New York College at Brockport. At SUNY Stony Brook, Shiming Hu rigorously taught me basic Chinese and together with Eli Seifman sustained my interest and guided my early research. Marcella Kysilka my doctoral advisor at the University of Central Florida helped me focus my dissertation. I appreciate your generous gifts of time and effort. Paul Fonoroff, good friend since our student days at Nanyang University in Singapore, helped me formulate arguments based on his remarkable perspective and knowledge about modern Chinese language, cinema and history. From the time we met at Fudan University, John and Ling Wu have taught me many things and helped translate articles from 1957 newspapers. I appreciate the efforts of Mr. Jun Tagami who painstakingly wrote the Chinese glossary for *Mao's Prey.*

I remain greatly indebted to the cooperation of Chinese and Americans who contributed oral histories and provided valuable insight concerning the fate of Chinese intellectuals. Chen Meida, Chen Renbing's sister explained the details of Chen's marriage break-up and other family matters. Correspondence from Li Wenyi, Chen's maternal aunt and leading member of the China Democratic League, clarified several important issues. Dr. Xie Xide, Smith and MIT educated physicist and past-President of Fudan University graciously allowed interviews at her Shanghai home. Dr. Tan Jiazhen, California Institute of Technology graduate, Fudan University geneticist and leading member of the China Democratic League, was one of the first intellectuals I interviewed. We met numerous times in 1981, 1982, 1992 and 1993. Former missionary Alma Pennypacker Wu, widow of a Chinese tuberculosis specialist explained the political movements after 1949 from the unique perspective of a foreigner living in China.

A Chinese musician, Wu Yiping, introduced me to Professor Ma Geshun, son of a Christian preacher, 1949 graduate of Westminster College choral conductor and retired Professor of the Shanghai Conservatory of Music. I will never forget the pain on Professor Ma's face when he told me the Cultural Revolution story of how he was beaten by a red guard. During a singing lesson Professor Ma suggested a student breathe as though "smelling a rose." The red guard slapped Professor Ma berating him saying, "You should tell your students to imagine they are smelling wheat, not a bourgeois flower!"

Tao Shaoyuan, University of Chicago graduate and Professor at Shanghai Teacher's College was in his nineties when he provided vivid details of Chinese Student Associations in the United States. I also had the great good fortune to meet and interview Mr. Lu Yi, wartime journalist and well-known newspaper editor who knew Chen Renbing well. In 1957 they were fellow rightists and inmates of the so-called "College of Socialism" reeducation camp in Shanghai .

In 1982, Fudan University arranged for me to meet several United States returned intellectuals who resided in Beijing. Among the dozen interviewees were Chen Daisun, Harvard-educated historian and retired Professor at Qinghua and Beijing Universities. Professor Sun had the distinction of being the first faculty member to return to Qinghua University after the Japanese occupation. Professor Tong Shibai, graduate of the University of Illinois and automation engineering professor at Qinghua University related his story of how difficult it was to return to China from the United States after diplomatic relations were broken after 1949.

Dr. Gordon Poteat (1891-1989) and his wife Helen Carruthers Poteat, contributed greatly to this study. They went to China in 1915 as missionaries with the Southern Baptist Church and I interviewed them dozens of times at their home in Ormond Beach, Florida. They were married for 70 years. Gordon's father was Dr. Edwin M. Poteat, president of Furman College from 1903-1918. The senior Poteat also went to China and both father and son were Chen Renbing's teachers. Gordon taught religion and Edwin taught philosophy at the Baptist supported University of Shanghai. Gordon and Helen Poteat's daughter Ann was also a classmate of Chen Renbing's. Chen Renbing and Ann Poteat performed in piano recitals as classmates.

Although Gordon Poteat is best known as pastor and author of the *Daily Devotional Series*, in 1924 he published *Home Letters From China*. In one letter, "On Adapting Preaching to China", Poteat commented on the missionary enterprise and conditions in early republican years of governmental decline and disintegration. Dr. Poteat emphasized the importance of economic independence for mission churches because "people ground into the dust by physical poverty cannot support a church in any country."(Poteat 109)

Chen Renbing met John Foster in 1938 as a colleague at Central China University in Wuchang. One of Dr. Chen's friends in Shanghai suggested I contact John Foster. John and Jane Foster wintered in Sarasota Florida and it was there that I met and interviewed them in 1992 and 1993. I am indebted to Professor Foster for providing crucial information from the unique point of view as an American in China sympathetic to the communist cause.

Foster taught at Central China University from 1934-1938 and for one semester took medical supplies to the Eighth Route Army in the Taihang Mountains in Shanxi. This was arranged by Agnes Smedley and Evans Carlson of the US Marines. Foster explained that his sponsor, the Episcopal Church, was not too happy about this activity and in 1939 he rejoined the college at its wartime location in Yunan.

Interviewees from Qinghua University and Beijing University provided crucial information and documents. Chinese friends affiliated with Fudan University and Shanghai Teachers University, helped locate and translate critical primary source documents, and explained so many things that I did not understand about the nature of Chinese politics and history. I listened and learned from famous professors and unknown scholars, most of them in the winter of their lives, yet some young and promising. Individually unique, collectively they always encouraged me to reveal details of what the intelligentsia had endured. The burden of public acknowledgment understood, I humbly proffer profound appreciation to all the anonymous voices who guided this work. Your names do not appear here but your efforts are indelibly etched in my heart.

My family and friends may not have shared my unwavering conviction of the project's importance yet they unstintingly supported my endeavors. Special thanks to the careful editing of my mother Rose Marie Ford and the patience of my husband Marcelo and children Kathleen, Mark and Claudia. The passion I feel for my family combined with the passion I maintain for this subject has not always been a comfortable mix. I regret not giving full attention to my work but decided that I was unwilling to take time away from my primary responsibilities. After all, children are only child-like temporarily whereas history is a constant treasury. Other scholars will devote time and energy to investigate questions that arise from this work, of that I am confident. In the meantime, should this volume serve to dust off the names of erstwhile intellectuals toward recognition of what might have been if not for the hardship and tragedy of wasted potential, a measure of satisfaction is realized.

All errors and omissions are my own. There is always more to be done.

Jeannette Ford Fernandez
March 2000
South Daytona, Florida

Foreword

The core of *Mao's Prey: The History of Chen Renbing, Liberal Intellectual* is oral history. Intellectuals have faced unique perils in modern Chinese history. Several individuals who contributed thoughts and remembrances prefer to remain nameless. I have respected their wishes and confirm that all the information is presented as it was to me by interview or letter.

Oftentimes meeting one intellectual led to acquaintance with another. At times, some of the respondent's rich background was unknown to the author. This is particularly true in the case of Mr. Sun Dayu, movie director, graduate of Qinghua and Yale universities, expert on Shakespeare and member of the Union of Democratic College Professors. Questions posed at his Shanghai residence in 1982 did not include crucial inquiries about being a major target of criticism during the Thought Reform Movement as writer and director of the movie Wu Hsun. Professor Sun was also capped in the 1957 Anti-Rightist Movement. Chen Renbing and Sun Dayu had been colleagues at St. John's University.

According to Theodore H.E. Chen in *Thought Reform of the Chinese Intellectuals,* Sun Yu was American trained and the story of Wu Hsun was at first lauded then used as a "weapon in the party's effort to indoctrinate Western-educated intellectuals in the party's political requirements". The accusations were that Sun portrayed Wu Hsun as exemplifying qualities the communist party was determined to eradicate. Wu Hsun was depicted as muddle-headed idealist who sought to change China through education and reform rather than through class struggle and revolution.

Chou Yang (the party leader who led the persecution of writers in the early-mid 1950s) pointed out that many intellectuals like the fictional Wu Hsun believe that "it is not necessary to have a revolutionary struggle of the people to overthrow the old system and establish a new one, it is only necessary to give people education and reform." (Chen 92)

To contradict this "nonprolitarian" thinking Chou Yang asserted that "Although we should emphasize education, we should not consider it above class and politics." Sun Yu published a public confession in the People's Daily newspaper on June 10, 1952. (Chen 92) I regret losing the opportunity to ask about Sun's experience of being criticized in a nation-wide campaign and how it affected his career.

Family members, friends and acquaintances spoke of Chen Renbing as a romantic idealist, a patriotic performer who risked and lost his career in the face of changing values. Some portray him as a naive 'eternal optimist', pure-hearted, yet vain who never passed up an opportunity to give patriotic speeches. Lu Yi in a July 9, 1992 interview in Shanghai at his Wu Kang Road home, described Chen Renbing's personality, as "very easy-going."

> He was influenced by American ideas. Chen cared for others, for example he followed the custom in the west of "ladies first." In a lot of situations, he thought about his friends, classmates and other people, and not for himself. He did not act for himself, he was not selfish like a lot of other people. He could have become an administrator, but he chose differently.
>
> Chen, a Hubei native who grew up in Wuhan, organized a song and dance troop and traveled to Southeast Asia performing anti-Japanese propaganda for overseas Chinese. His work had a big influence before liberation when he joined the people's movements. Chen taught at St. John's University and in the eyes of the students he was very respected. Chen was patriotic and was against Japan.
>
> In 1937 he did a lot of very dangerous things for the China Democratic League, then an underground movement. He could sing songs and also played the flute very well. We were of the same heart. We certainly did not look down on the peasants or workers. We could all work together. We should not be put in the same category as old men of the party who tell lies. Professor Chen Ren Bing also was very humorous. In cultural aspects, he was very talented.

A professor friend of Chen's for more than 50 years, who wishes to remain anonymous, arranged for him to earn some money during the lean years of the Cultural Revolution by doing translations. In a series of interviews in the summer of 1992, the professor told a weird tale of his own serious trouble during the Cultural Revolution.

The professor's nephew by marriage tried to extricate himself from Public Security Bureau interrogation by claiming the professor had been head of the Ku Klux Klan while studying in the United States! Furthermore, he alleged his uncle was hoarding gold bars under his apartment floor! These absurd accusations caused his apartment to be torn apart and nearly resulted in the professor being executed. The professor's opinion was that Chen Renbing, however flawed, was a true representative the Chinese intellectual tradition.

> We became friends when we went to St. John's University. He was the head of the college of humanities there. We were at St. John's for a year. When St. John's closed (during educational reorganization), we waited for half a year and then both of us were transferred to Fudan University and stayed there ever since. I think Renbing's main trouble was that he was too outspoken. The whole family was (designated as Rightists), his father, his younger brother.

> It is natural for Chinese intellectuals to be outspoken to say what is right. He was never a yes-man. He didn't like the present democratic parties to be yes-men to the Communist party. No! That kind of attitude could never be tolerated and he could never be a yes-man. Chen Renbing did not see himself as a member of the opposition party but found something he could speak differently about. Was Chen Renbing expected to be a leader and not just sit back? Yes, because in the period of the revolution before liberation he was outspoken all the time.

> Chen had a tremendous love for vanity. That was his weak point and he was attacked on a charge of being immoral. He became notorious because at the time we met he was living with a woman that was his (paternal) aunt. He was having dancing parties and in a lot of trouble. The officials called them 'dim light parties'. One of the third secretaries of the (Communist) Party of Fudan University who handled the History Department faculty members cases in 1957, accused Chen of holding immoral dancing parties where the women were not wearing panties. But this of course was completely false. Chen was dismissed from the professorial rank and deprived of the title of member of the faculty. Then his salary reflected the carpenter's salary.

> I have met Chen's father and mother. His father was very famous you know. Every time a church man came to China to visit Chairman Mao, his father was on the site. Chen's father did not have any of his son's vanity.

Chapter I: Introduction

In 1980, a story circulated in Shanghai about Dr. Chen Renbing[1] (1919-1990) and was recalled by Jane Foster, wife of a visiting American scholar:

> In the afternoon, one of John's old friends, a teacher of sociology[2] turned up. He stayed over 3 hours, telling us the tale of his life. John had last seen him in Penang in 1940 when John was enroute from Rangoon to Hong Kong. Chen was an activist in support of the left and Democratic League in those days—a fourth generation Christian. His father was a minister of the Swedish-American church.
>
> In 1947, his first wife and two daughters left China for the United States and he had not seen them since. This man had an MA from the University of Southern California and Ph.D. from the University of Michigan. In 1957, he was labeled a 'Capitalist Roader' (He was personally named by Mao Zedong as being an anti-Communist party "Rightist" and was vilified and punished, or "capped"[3]) and has done no teaching since. At first he had been dean at St. John's University and later professor at Fudan. Chen lost his rank and salary and for 9 years worked in a carpenter's shop at Fudan. Since last June he has been allowed to teach again but still is not "uncapped." His father, younger brother and self were all declared "Rightists." Another brother, a doctor, was beaten to death during the Cultural Revolution (1966-1976), had seven ribs broken and his death was not revealed till 5 years after the fact. Another brother, a physicist, was put to hard physical labor and died as a result.
>
> Chen and wife divorced and he married again in 1964 and has a 17-year old son. He also has a step-daughter by wife's first marriage. Next week, he starts teaching again at Fudan. During the years, there has

been a tremendous amount of ostracism. But it seems the "capped" have stuck together and given each other moral support. For years, he lived on 57[4] yuan a month, reduced from 220 yuan but now is getting some of his pay back. This is one of the most horrendous stories I have heard.[5]

In 1992, John Foster[6] wondered, "why the family should have been on somebody's blacklist?" Professor Foster said, "I have a number of Chinese friends in the same boat, some of whom have enjoyed high office in the People's Republic. Chen Renbing came to be my colleague in September 1936[7]. I always understood that he and his wife disagreed on where they wanted to live, Mrs. Chen wanting to bring up the children in a peaceful environment and Dr. Chen wanting to throw in his lot with his war-torn country."[8]

Why did Chen Renbing go to the United States for advanced academic degrees? What compelled him to return to a China in the throes of civil war and Japanese invasion? What happened to him and other Chinese intellectuals after they returned to China? What is the relationship between intellectuals and the communist government? The answers to these questions reveal the importance of intellectual scholarship in the first half of this century to the development of China.

The story of what happened during 1920s and 1930s and World War II and its aftermath to the overseas trained intellectuals and the role they played in China's history after World War II can be told through the recollections of Chen Renbing and the overseas educated. They reflected on their lives as intellectuals in China during the rise and implementation of communism and anti-intellectual movements, including the Thought Reform Movement, the Anti-Rightist Movement, the Cultural Revolution and the downfall of the Gang of Four and an attempt to return to a more civil society.

The data to answer the question of "intellectuals" influence during these times is revealed through interviews and documents. Early interviews for this study gathered from 1980-1982 were subjected to conditions enforced because some of the interview sessions were arranged, monitored, and censored by Fudan, Beijing or Qinghua University officials and Communist party officials. Access was restricted to approximately three dozen intellectuals willing to be interviewed and therefore present a version which may or may not reveal the earlier story.

Some interviews were conducted at private residences. A few individuals allowed multiple interviews, however, Chen Renbing unfolded his entire life story during frequent meetings at his home for several months in 1981-82 and by correspondence until his death in 1990. Eldest son of a famous Christian minister, Chen had sociology degrees from the University of Southern California (MA, 1932) and the University of Michigan at Ann

Arbor (Ph.D., 1936) Later, in the United States, several Americans who taught, studied with or knew Dr. Chen were interviewed.

Chen's own account, based on his more open and demonstrative personal style, were validated by later interviews conducted in the summer of 1992, and fall 1993, when I was a lecturer at Shanghai Teacher's University.

These mostly male intellectuals provided fascinating details of their early lives and education abroad. However, even more questions arose with the realization that their influence upon returning to China was severely limited by anti-intellectual mass political movements.

Why were intellectuals targeted for punishment after answering Mao's call to speak out for Communist party reform in 1957? Why were they prevented from fulfilling a role that for a millennium has been the mainstay of Chinese culture and politics? If educated people are traditionally respected in China, how could intellectuals be branded "serpent spirits and oxen devils" during the Cultural Revolution 1966-1976? How many died defending themselves, how many died at their own hands? What series of events led to wholesale discrediting of the intellectual elite of the world's most populous nation?

Answers to questions about why the influence of American-returned intellectuals was denied in China were found through oral history interviews and research conducted on the history of the study abroad phenomenon and primary source material gathered to determine what happened to intellectuals after 1949 and why intellectuals became Mao's prey.

A segment of the story lies in the influence that United States scholars had on the growth and development of democratic ideals in China. As more Chinese students went to the United States for advanced degrees, they became acquainted first hand with Western scholarship and a lifestyle guided by the ideology inherent in the American constitution. Of pivotal influence is scholarship integral to intellectual development being promulgated on Chinese soil. For two years, from 1919 to 1921 during the so-called 'Chinese Renaissance' John Dewey lectured extensively and was considered a faculty member at Beijing University and Qinghua Preparatory College. Charting the impact teachers and missionaries from the United States had on their students as evidenced in the oral histories of intellectuals provides chilling evidence of the link between pro-Western learning and the ugly consequences of being targeted by Mao Zedong as a "stinking intellectual."

The whole story may not be totally revealed until much later in history. This is an attempt at making part of the story public beyond the borders of China.

ORIGINS OF THE STUDY ABROAD PHENOMENON

In the 4,000 year long course of Chinese ideological and cultural development, China has been relatively isolated from the rest of the world. Buoyed by ideas usually characterized by their close connections with the ethical practices in daily life, focus traditionally was on personal morality and the maxim of social ethics. Neighboring countries paid tribute to the "Middle Kingdom" and followed the Chinese example of civilization and modernity, copying Chinese style of writing and government. From an intellectual and cultural viewpoint, Chinese science and ideas, undoubtedly at a high level throughout the medieval period in world history had begun falling behind the West since the Renaissance.[10]

The central theme of modern Chinese history has been to learn to compete with the West so as to gain a foothold in the modern world. In the transformation to study western learning to achieve national prosperity and strength in modern times, China made a tremendous effort and paid dearly. Western learning spread in the beginning of this century, however the concepts of the rights and of the rule of law went against feudal social relationships.

In modern times China was surpassed by other countries[11] and began to be looked upon as a place to plunder. Instead of respecting the emperor and paying tribute, foreigners imported drugs and sought to impose their customs and commerce. China's weakening was compounded by the international communities acceptance of the terms of pivotal historical events, the Opium Wars, the Boxer Rebellion and the Versailles Treaty.

In the 1800s, the Qing Dynasty government (1644-1911) decided to punish the English and eradicate opium imports which resulted in widespread and pernicious addiction and drained Chinese silver currency. Imperial Commissioner Lin Zexu was dispatched to engage the British in a public controversy over imports. Lin vigorously opposed importing opium yet he favored trade and welcomed law-abiding foreigners. Lin argued that Chinese must study world relations and conditions and train talented people for the future particularly since the Qing government did not understand the West[12]. Change invariably creates chaos, Lin warned, and people must be prepared for changes in law and create policies molded for evolving needs. Commissioner Lin compared his thoughts that world struggles varied to the changing temperatures of winter and summer. His progressive outlook derived from comparisons between China and Western countries and his knowledge of Chinese classics and ancient history.

China attempted a show of strength but was no match for England in two wars to stop opium imports. Just after the first Opium War, a reformer[13] argued that the very people who do not understand things are the ones who sign the agreements. His criticism was a specific reference to the August 29, 1842 Nanjing Treaty which gave Britain an indemnity, dismantled trade monopolies, opened five trading ports, surrendered Hong Kong, granted equal official status to British diplomats and determined fixed tariffs.

Weak economic conditions[14] and deep shame over China's defeats fomented discontent of peasants already tottering on the brink of starvation. This was particularly true in southern China far distant from the Qing capital. Around 1850, Hong Xiuquan led a major uprising, the Taiping Rebellion, by adopting quasi-Christian tenants of human equality to recruit soldiers of both sexes. Droves of poor peasants joined Hong's 'kingdom of heavenly peace' and conquered vast areas of China over a 14-year period.

The heavenly kingdom platform[15] which promised to abolish opium, foot binding and bride buying, recognize equality of the sexes, institute free trade and introduce primitive communism, was never put into practice because the changes were beyond what popular tradition would endure. Control remained among the powerful, and, even though land was equally distributed, there was no true land reform.

In March 1862 the Qing government relied on modern British and American weaponry and military techniques to defeat the rebels. The foreigners were eager to assist the dynasty because they feared victorious Taiping leaders would likely forbid the sale of opium, rescind treaties and not maintain privileges granted to them by the Qing government. Thus, although the Qing handily overcame the peasant uprising they could not forestall eventual decline.

As the Qing dynasty faced demise, it unsuccessfully adopted a few modern ideas of jurisprudence. The attempt to abolish feudal codes conveyed a sense that the democratic tide of the time could not be stopped.[16]

From 1862 to 1874 the conservative Qing court acquiesced to demands by a small group of liberal Chinese statesmen in the Self Strengthening Movement and created a Foreign Affairs Bureau in 1861. Yale University graduate Rong Hong[17] suggested that Chinese boys be sent to America to study science and technology. Upon their return, it was hoped they could work toward overcoming obstacles in China. Rong was made Commissioner of the Chinese Educational Mission and in 1872, 120 Chinese boys age 10 to 16 went to the United States and another 30 were sent to England and France for technical training. The candidates had 6 months of preliminary training in Shanghai and were subject to strict standards and requirements.

Over a 10 to 15-year period in the United States, participants studied engineering, mathematical or military subjects, continued classical Chinese studies and were examined annually by Mission tutors. Armed with modern knowledge, students were supposed to return to China and put their western training to use in government service. However, fierce criticism greeted reports that students failed to adhere to staid Confucian standards. Rong's students played baseball, dated American girls and even adopted

Christianity. Claiming moral decline, the Qing Court recalled the entire body of Mission students in 1881. Only two boys finished degrees, the others were in high school or just beginning college.

As this first wave of overseas students returned, education in China began a dramatic change. Prior to 1878 there were no Western-type schools in China except those conducted by foreign missionaries. Existing schools were all privately supported by families or philanthropic individuals, or more often, were conducted by private teachers on their own initiative as a means of livelihood. In 1902, a new educational era in China saw the first school code issued by the Emperor[18]. Wide in scope with a number of and variety of institutions proposed, it required 21 years to pass from the lowest primary through university, 17 through college and 14 through high school.

The main objective of such schools was to prepare candidates for passing the series of competitive civil service examinations. Traditional exams were open to all classes of male citizens and constituted a path to high social standing and political power. However, the exam system was abolished[19] when the Qing dynasty was overthrown in 1911, leaving the Chinese little time to create their own advanced degree system to determine the ranks of intellectuals.

One solution was to bring in a ready-made product from the West, a foreign education. Chinese began to follow Japan's example and used Western learning to promulgate democratic ideas.[20] When the loss of the 1884 Sino-Japanese War stimulated a great transformation among Chinese intellectuals it caused progressives extreme distress and indignation. The threat of national subjugation and genocide was imminent, and demands for a way to ensure China's survival included a call for Western learning, reform and modernization, and human rights and equality.

Humiliation, hardship, and political corruption were common pressures on a people denied development in the absence of armed conflict. Since the decade before the dynasty fell, major Chinese cities had completely autonomous foreign concessions where English, French, American, Japanese and other non-Chinese nationalities lived. Chinese disputed the authority of the Shanghai Municipal Council of the Foreign Concessions to enforce so-called "Oriental Law", an unwritten mixture of customs and precedent which followed a general policy of unhindered growth in the concessions.

Foreign businesses enjoyed more favorable conditions owing to the existence of specific commercial legislation. Chinese businessmen, hampered by an anachronistic non-democratic judicial system, had to adapt to unfamiliar European and American legalities based on the influence of the French Revolution and the Declaration of Independence.

Frustrations grew and the Boxer Rebellion of 1900, a primitive form of a patriotic peasant uprising occurred. The motive was to oust foreigners but the method of attacking and destroying much of the foreign legations in Beijing backfired. As a result, foreigners allied to infringe upon Chinese sovereignty and occupied the city. An enormous indemnity of $330 million was demanded in reparations to Russia, Germany, France, Britain, Japan, USA, Italy, Belgium, Austria and others.

This served to inhibit China's economic growth, strengthened the foreign diplomatic corps, and exposed China in an uncivilized light in the community of nations. China was forced to turn to revolution as the only hope for national salvation in light of the dynasty's weakness.[21]

In Beijing, Qinghua Preparatory College, nicknamed "Indemnity College", was established in 1909 when the Roosevelt administration returned monies China paid as indemnity for damages to the American legation. The college's unique feature was that it was built American style, and staffed mostly by an American faculty.

Qinghua dispatched the next large scale organized group of Chinese students to the United States. From 1911 on, the college admitted at least 100 students annually for a minimum 2-year college course as preparation for their studies abroad. The curriculum heavily emphasized English language, Western studies, and rigorous physical exercise, something new to Chinese students. Before graduates were sent to America, they were expected to give lectures in English, hold debates and pass a swimming test.[22]

In 1914, Qinghua Preparatory College began accepting women as candidates, provided they did not have bound feet. The women did not study at the Qinghua Preparatory College campus near Beijing, but rather took exams to qualify them as overseas scholarship recipients. Until 1925, all graduates were sent to the United States to complete advanced degrees. Young students were awarded scholarships based on nationwide yearly exams and pursued an 8-year course. Excerpts from a letter written by a Chinese student in the United States on November 20, 1919, and published in the Qinghua Student Weekly reveals the depth of a student's patriotic devotion.

> People here are very kind to the Chinese and it is easy for us to make friends, for they welcome us everywhere. The only defect is, they know very little about China. In the first place, the books concerning the subject are very few and in the second place, they were written mostly by missionaries some 10 or 20 years ago. There are some books written by the Japanese about their own country. So people here seem to know more and better about Japan, and many people call us Japanese. They know about the Shandong questions but very little about the true aspect. When we talk with them and tell them what it really is, they will say, "Is that so! Then Japan is wrong." So, it is the fault of the Chinese Students, I think, for not being able to translate or write books about the real conditions of China. I have made some new acquaintances either in the classes or in the YMCA and they complain about the same thing. Whenever we meet, they will be glad to know China

from me. Sometimes, we talk after class and forget to go home. We both realize that in this way we know the likeness and unlikeness of different people and progress in social development may result. It is a special delight to me, because I was taught in Qinghua and I personally believe that is why I can benefit myself by coming to this country.[23]

THE MAY FOURTH MOVEMENT

The "Shandong Question" alluded to by the student refers to the infamous Japanese 'Twenty One Demands' of the Versailles Conference in 1915. Japan was granted succession to German rights in Shangdong Province, extension to 99 years of the leases in southern Manchuria with commercial freedom for Japanese living there, half interest in a certain iron and steel mills and a declaration that no part of China's coast should be leased or ceded to any other foreign power. These ultimatums were presented in secrecy to Chinese delegates at Versailles who agreed to sign modified versions. Their actions caused a humiliating national crisis.

Infuriated Chinese sparked resistance efforts and guided a powerful consensus among people in all parts of the country. On May 4, 1919, Beijing University students organized to present petitions for the Paris negotiating conference to foreign legations. The protest swelled and turned violent when protesters passed the home of one of the traitorous Versailles delegates.

The demonstrators forced their way into the home. The Chinese Minister to Japan who had agreed to Japan's secret demands was assaulted and his house set on fire. Police arrested 10 students. Enraged citizens demanded release of the 10 and destroyed or boycotted Japanese goods. A general strike ensued, and a former government minister, then Chancellor of Peking University[24] resigned in protest.

On May 7, the students were released and the Chinese delegation eventually yielded to the people's demands and rejected the secret treaty made with the Japanese. Excerpts from the weekly newsletters vividly recount student involvement in political events.

Even before the events of May 4, 1919 unfolded, the Qinghua University English Supplement weekly of Thursday April 18, 1919 notes the formation of the "The North China Western Returned Students' Association." One of the Association's "extremely important decisions" was to "send telegrams to "Peace Delegations of France, Great Britain, Italy and the United States, and, to the Chinese Peace Delegation" at the Versailles Conference. The returned students "called for a united China, abolition of the military system and (a measure) prohibiting soldiers and military officers from interfering with political affairs."[25]

The students wrote, "We believe that Democracy is the best form of government for China", and pleaded for "education of the masses", "freedom of speech and publication", "governmental reforms along the line of modern efficiency, especially with regard to greater responsibility in financial administration and the actual adoption of the civil service system and unifying the currency system." The telegrams ended with the statement, "We stand for the abrogation of the so-called 'spheres of influence' and 'spheres of interest' in China."[26]

On May 9, 1919, the Qinghua Weekly records "a great mass meeting in memory of our National Disgrace of 1915 was held in the gymnasium. Besides all the (Chinese) teachers, members of the staff, students, servants and cooks, all the American teachers were also present." The program included patriotic speeches, reading the Twenty-One Demands of 1915, saluting the national flag and singing the national song. Officers of the student commission read the recent telegram from our Chinese delegates at Paris and, "after this, all came out and assembled around a great heap of Japanese goods (both of the college store and of some students) which was consequently burned amidst patriotic shouts and cheers."

> In order to arouse the spirit of common people, the delegates from all the schools decided to send a number of small groups of students to all parts of Peking, lecturing to the public and distributing leaflets. It is said that more than 20,000 leaflets were distributed.[27]

A Qinghua College delegate was dispatched to Tianjin to persuade Mr. Cai Yuanpei to return to his post as President of Peking Government University. Beginning May 5, the Weekly published an Extra Special edition twice a day, so as to keep the student-body well informed of the current news both inside and outside the college.

> The Student's Union followed a policy to attack and impeach all traitors, start a daily newspaper to arouse the patriotic spirit in the common people, to dispatch telegrams to all schools and colleges in China informing them of the situation and asking them to follow our movement. Send delegates to all provinces, organize a National Student Federation, influence all classes of people, especially the merchant class, not to use Japanese bank notes. Influence all newspapers not to advertise Japanese trade and commerce and secure help from the Chamber of Commerce as a backing force.[28]

Fund-raising activities to meet expenses of the student commission were raised by contributions and reduction of student's regular boarding fees. "Servants also contributed" small sums and "all regular classes of the servant night school have now been temporarily turned into special lectures so to give the servants a good idea of the present critical situation and thereby arouse their patriotic spirit. The same thing has been introduced into the Sunday School of the Confucian Association."[29]

Further efforts were aimed to "Unite all returned students and students abroad, hold a mass meeting and grand demonstration in Beijing and, introduce military training in all schools." Student activists planned to "canvass the Parliament, cut off necessary supplies from China to Japan, get into close touch with every Provincial Assembly and send telegrams to all parts of China to boycott Japanese goods."[30]

In addition, "every student (was asked) to write letters home explaining this great and worthy movement" Qinghua students "lectured in the streets of Peking every day" and arranged to send delegates all over China. They "requested one of our graduates or any other man who is now in France to represent us there and to get into close touch with the (Versailles Conference delegate).[31] Students proposed to "unite with all Chinese students in America" as well.

Determined not to miss any possible contacts, the Qinghua Student Commission urgently requested that every student write a letter to his mother-school or his old school-mates requesting them to follow the movement and send articles to both Chinese and foreign newspapers to declare the real patriotic attitude of the Chinese people.

When students gave lectures and distributed leaflets, they reminded everyone of the National Disgrace of 1915, and planned to "organize a permanent organization, erect a memorial of some kind and print words or expression on all electric wire poles." Furthermore, "a standing committee (would) carry on the work during the summer vacation and organize sub-headquarters in every province in the summer to get every student into some kind of work."[32]

JOHN DEWEY AND HU SHI

The May Fourth Movement's anti-Japanese boycott rapidly spread over China. Professor John Dewey arrived to lecture as one of the first United States scholars who began to populate China and cause a new way of thinking to emerge. Dewey stayed in China for 2 years, and a contemporary wrote,

> A factor which exerted a very great influence on educational opinion
> was the work of Drs. John Dewey (1859-1952) and Paul Monroe, of
> Columbia University, New York, whose lectures and magazine articles
> on the philosophy of education and educational administration during
> their visits in China aroused great interest and were widely discussed
> by the newspapers, and in the schools.[33]

Dr. Hu Shi, (1891-1962) scion of a famous early Qing scholar, graduated from Cornell and Columbia universities. He served as interpreter for his professor John Dewey and profoundly influenced intellectuals at a time when Chinese education was altered in content, methods and diffusion. Hu developed a new style of writing called "bai wen" or "plain speech" that was close to colloquial speech and far easier to use and read than the terse unpunctuated classical style that was de rigueur for earlier generation of reformers.

'Bai wen' became accepted for scholarly and practical purposes. Punctuation facilitated understanding of both ancient and modern texts. Preparation of indexes made works widely accessible.

A flood of periodicals, quarterly, monthly and weekly, afforded a medium for scholarly publication and interchange of current views almost totally lacking before. From 1912 to 1922, a process of evolution and a development of initiative was steadily moving forward within schools and the influence of returned students from America was gradually becoming stronger.

Hu Shi firmly believed in pragmatism, scientific methods of thought and the evolutionary improvement of society. Because of the Thomas Huxley and Dewey influences, the main sources of Hu's inspiration were agnosticism and pragmatism, which became his principal approaches in evaluating traditional ethics and ideas. Truth, according to the pragmatist, is changeable in proportion to its utility based on experimentation. Such an attitude, distinctly a product of an industrial capitalistic society, was diametrically opposed to the Confucian concept that thought is eternal and unchangeable. Hu considered Confucianism totally out of touch with modern world realities and he invented the pejorative phrase 'Confucius and Sons Incorporated,' and his followers shouted, 'Down with Confucianism.'[34]

"Hu was against Confucianism, he was for liberalism, individualism, science and democracy. Drawing from pragmatism, he preached a gradual, bit-by-bit improvement of society through study of its problems, experimentation, and solution. Under his aegis, "Mr. Science" and "Mr. Democracy" became the catchwords of the age. Since both originated in the West, Hu in effect advocated a complete Westernization. "Go West!" was his message. Hu's philosophy is best explained in his own words:

> The spirit of the new thought tide is a critical attitude. The methods of the new thought tide are the study of problems and the new introduction of academic theories...The attitude of the new thought tide toward the old civilization is, on the negative side, to oppose blind obedience and oppose compromise, and on the positive side, to reorganize our national heritage with scientific methods. What is the sole aim of the new thought tide? It is to recreate civilization.[35]

Dr. Hu Shi spoke against Confucianism, yet respected philosopher John Dewey who auspiciously celebrated his 60th birthday just around the same time of year as Confucius' birthday, was lauded as a modern day sage. Hu Shi objected to the feudal origins of the Confucian code of a cosmic order and its hierarchy of superior-inferior relationships. Hu rejected these notions which resulted in a social and political context of esteem for age over youth, of the past over the present, for established authority over innovation and the overall conservative outlook.[36]

Hu Shi tried to avoid politics as he tried to make people understand that nation-building meant China had to abandon ancient ideologies. Confucius as problem-solver was acceptable, however the very tenets of Confucian philosophy perpetuated class relationships. Even Mao Zedong evoked the positive image of Confucius when praising a modern Chinese writer Lu Xun. "As for Lu Xun's worth in China, he is in my view a Chinese sage of the first rank. If Confucius was the sage of feudal China, Lu Xun is the sage of modern China."[37]

In 1924, American missionary Dr. Gordon Poteat wrote of a "recent attempt in China to make Confucianism the state religion. The common people were held in the fetters of superstition; exercising their vague religious feelings in ways they could not explain except on the basis of custom—because our forefathers did so."[38] The Confucianist opposition argued that Jesus is an outsider come to overthrow the doctrines of 3 millenniums. Jesus is declared to be greater than Confucius and claims to be divine. Put Jesus on the same plane with Confucius and little is said against him...It is common to hear speeches nowadays on ethics and virtue in which Christ is placed in the gallery of the sages, equal but not higher than the rest."[39]

"Dr. Hu Shi says that Confucianism was never intended to be a world religion, even though it is the most important cultural influence in the evolution of China. It was never a religion with missionaries—Mencius, the greatest Confucianist philosopher, second only to Confucius in influence, once said, "Man's trouble lies in his desire to become a teacher of other men." And it is often said in Confucian literature that "courtesy demands that the pupils come to their teachers; and no teacher should go out to his pupils."[40]

Dewey's *The School and Society* (1899), and *Democracy and Education* (1916), received exposure in China. His comprehensive system of thought emphasizing the biological and social basis of knowledge and the instrumental character of ideas as plans of action, or, "experimental naturalism", became popular. He further developed the pragmatic school of thought as a principle of grounding knowledge on experience and stressing the inductive procedures of experimental science.[41]

Philosopher and psychologist William James, developed the pragmatic theory of truth as the capacity of a belief to guide one to successful action and proposed that all beliefs be evaluated in terms of their usefulness in solving problems. Dewey followed James as a leader of the pragmatic movement in philosophy and Dewey's own philosophy stems from the pragmatism of James and pragmatic idealism espoused by Josiah Royce which combined idealism with elements of pragmatism.

Dewey lectured at the National University in Peking and other universities. Some of his talks were titiled "Social and Political Philosophy," "The Philosophy of Education," "Ethics," "Types of Thinking," "Modern Trends in Education," and "Democratic Developments in America." The lectures were delivered in English, simultaneously interpreted in Chinese and recorded manually for use by the daily press and leading periodicals.[43]

At a banquet given by the 'warlord' governor of Hunan province, John Dewey first met the eminent British philosopher Bertrand Russell. Russell had landed in Shanghai a few weeks before, responding to an invitation by the Chinese Lecture Association to spend a year in China. After Bertrand Russell arrived in Peking, he and Dewey frequently met for informal philosophical discussions. Sometimes they were joined by other philosophers at Peking University.

Russell remained an acquaintance of Dewey's until they both departed in July 1921. Russell collapsed with pneumonia during his stay and was so critically ill that his obituary was prematurely printed in a British newspaper. Russell's lectures initially appealed to a more radical element in Chinese politics than did Dewey's. Many were frustrated however, when Russell insisted upon the value of China's great tradition of pacifist thought and praised such men as Lao Tzu.[44]

One account states that during Dewey's visit to a dying Russell in Peking in 1921, Russell outlined plans for ending national disputes. He and Dewey avidly discussed the situation in China and Russell debated with the leader of the Chinese Communist Party, Chen Duxu. These debates gripped China's intellectuals and influenced the young Mao Zedong and Zhu De.[45]

As a political activist, Dewey advocated progressive and sometimes radical approaches to international affairs and economic problems. In the 1920s, Dewey favored United States involvement in military actions and supported the League of Nations.[46]

During the fall semester of 1919, Dewey gave a series of lectures to high school students. On "Ethics," he stated that "the emotions have an intellectual element, to the extent of being aroused by an idea or image, as instincts do not."[47] He went on to say that of "the social emotions...patriotism is a mixture and couples social emotion, blended of gregariousness, sympathy, pride and attachment. (There is a) positive value in leading to public spirit, or preference of the wider good to the narrower is obvious. It may, however, be so manipulated as to take the form of suspicion and hostility to other social groups or people."[48]

Dewey spoke[49] to Qinghua Preparatory School students on "selfishness" emphasizing "the need to cultivate the natural sympathies and affections in an intellectual or intelligent form. That is, to transform them into habits of thinking about the ends and interests and capacities of others as if they were one's own. He defined "unselfishness (as meaning) wideness of outlook, breadth of vision, instead of narrowness and exclusiveness."

A few days later Professor Dewey presented another lecture entitled "Regard for Self and For Others." Continuing his weekly afternoon lectures, Professor Dewey spoke about "virtues and vices" emphasizing that "intelligence and emotion are not rivals."[50]

Dewey's effect on Chinese intellectuals reached beyond education, philosophy and psychology because there is a discernible thread connecting those boys who subsumed Dewey's ideas and the men who were persecuted by Mao Zedong.

Did Dewey offer a strategy that would be politically effective in the context of Chinese reform? No, Dewey lectured, acted as an educational consultant, and studied educational systems in China,[51] emphasizing how ideas can work in everyday life, how logic and philosophy varied and could be adapted to need and circumstance. For Dewey, the thinking process was a means of planning action, of removing the obstacles between what is given and what is wanted. Truth is an idea that has worked in practical experience. He insisted on an experimental approach to ethics, on relating values to individual and social needs.[52]

Deweyan educational principles emphasized learning through varied activities rather than formal curricula and opposed authoritarian methods which offered contemporary people no realistic preparation for life in a democratic society. Dewey felt, moreover, that education should not merely be a preparation for future life but a full life in itself.[53]

That intellectuals would prepare themselves for creative activity in a democratic society was an idea that caused Chen Renbing in particular and western-trained intellectuals in general to be persecuted in anti-intellectual campaigns.

Dewey's work and his writings were largely responsible for the drastic change in pedagogy that began in the United States early in the 20th century. In China, owning to the ideological underpinnings of Marxist-Leninist-Mao Zedong Thought, the Deweyan effect has been to identify pro-Western intellectuals as Mao's prey. We will see how the fodder for accusations against Hu and Dewey were laid in the 1920s and 1930s.

POLITICAL ACTIVIST LUO LONGJI

Chen Renbing and others who returned from overseas study during the republican era were looked upon as leaders. Their western acquired learning provided academic degrees which supplanted the tradition within China's dynastic history of high office being granted to those who passed complex examinations.

China's unstable political climate provided an environment whereby intellectuals became the purveyors of new ideas and fresh ideologies. They used the popular press to promulgate ideas. Therefore, certain intellectuals became well known to the literate public and young people were drawn to a variety of public figures like Luo Longji.

Luo Longji (1898-1965) was a native of Anfu County Jiangsu Province. Luo attended Dewey's lectures and figured prominently in the May Fourth Movement activities as a student at Qinghua Preparatory College.

At Qinghua Preparatory College Luo served in the reorganized Student Commission as one of "five representatives to draw up the constitution" elected by the Junior class.[54] Luo spent 8 years at Qinghua and was president of the Qinghua Student Union and Chief Editor of the Qinghua Weekly. Mr. Luo placed second with a speech on "Chinese Returned Students" and the Chinese Oratorical and Debating Society elected Luo president.[55] Later, Luo was re-elected as president of the Society and chief executive officers of the Qinghua Student Organization formally established Luo as speaker.[56]

Luo spent a year studying at the London School of Economics, and, in 1928, earned a Ph.D. at Columbia University. Chen Renbing was well acquainted with Luo's writing and political philosophy and consistently credited Luo as his political mentor.

Dr. Luo was well known for activities in organizing student cliques and conducting student movements.[57] Luo and Hu Shi were contemporaries with very different ideas of political participation. Hu Shi's

> experience suggests certain exceptions to generally held about the course of liberalism in modern China....it had been observed, especially in the case of Hu Shi, the foremost Chinese disciple of John Dewey and the most renowned upholder of the liberal standard in the May Fourth era, that China's Western-trained intellectuals exhibited a distaste for politics narrowly understood, preferring to find in professional careers a public relevance. Despite a deep appreciation for freedom, intellectual pluralism, and their accompanying political frameworks, they remained skeptical, if not disdainful, of the rough and tumble of political activism. This general observation does not apply to Lo. An intensely political person from his days as a student leader at Qinghua college in the May Fourth era through his attempt to question the Chinese Communist Party monopoly 4 decades later in the hundred flowers period, Lo never withdrew from the public arena to pursue a private calling. On the contrary, a principal message he sought to bring to his audience among students and intellectuals was the urgency of political engagement.[58]

Luo gained notoriety as a student activist at Qinghua. As president of the student union and editor of the Qinghua student weekly, he played a leading role in the May Fourth demonstrations and the student strikes that followed. Luo boasted in later years, "Nine years at Qinghua, three school presidents dismissed."[59] Although in the 1930s he beseeched the new generation of students to fulfill their academic responsibilities, he never questioned the value of student activism.

This is a significant point of departure from the position of Hu Shi, with whom he had collaborated in articulating and defending human rights in the pages of New Month magazine.

As Dean at Beijing University in the mid-1930s, Hu urged students to recognize that, at a time of national crisis, their foremost responsibility was to develop their knowledge and abilities. He cautioned against mass demonstrations and actions which violated the spirit of the age, warning students to be wary of minority manipulation."[60]

Later in life, Luo Longji asserted that individual freedom would lead to a strengthening of the nation. This is an argument shared by Liang Qichao, and the British thinker Harold Laski, Luo's teacher at the London School of Economics.[61] Moreover, influenced by Confucianism, the liberals tended to stress the worth of the individual.

Chen was drawn to Luo Longji's notion that linked a Western-inspired outlook with total political engagement. Chen's devotion to political activities embodied the belief that an individual could privately follow his personal calling and still have a public significance.

Dr. Luo served as President of the Association of Chinese Students in America in 1937. Overseas students typically belonged to Chinese student associations, fraternities or sororities while in the USA and kept close fraternal ties upon their return to China. Some of Chen Renbing's pivotal ties in China reflected his membership in the "Flip Flap" fraternity, named after a Broadway show by an earlier group of Chinese students.

Funds necessary to travel and study in the United States were provided by family or other private means. If money was provided by the Nationalist government it was expected to be paid back by government service upon the students return to China.

After his return to China, Dr. Luo taught at various universities and was very active in the China Democratic League. "From 1932-1942, he was a member of the Nationalist People's Political Council and joined the Political Consultative Conference in 1946. According to Chen Renbing, Luo Longji created the motto for the Korean campaign, "To Protect Home and Country." In the Communist government, he was awarded appointment as minister of timber in 1956[62] because of his position as a respected economist with strong political clout.

Luo Longji and Hu Shi were contemporaries with very different ideas of political participation. Fredric J. Spar observed that especially in the case of intellectuals like Hu, there was exhibited a distaste for politics narrowly understood, preferring to find in professional careers a public relevance.[63] Luo penned prolific editorials aimed at the student audience in the Tianjin and Beijing area.

We will see how Luo Longji became infamous in his lifetime as an early target in the Anti-rightist Campaign of 1957 and how Chen Renbing, Luo's political protégé and close friend, was snared in the same purge. In a general sense, Chen Renbing, like his mentor, enjoyed the 'rough and tumble of political activism' and Chen displayed a penchant for public speaking and celebrity even in his youth.

Chen's early education among foreign missionaries within a Christian school compound, his father's global view, and Chen's experience studying in the United States resulted in Chen's lifelong espousal of democracy and individual rights.

Chen Renbing provided a unique glimpse into the social circles and political experiences of the intellectual elite in China. Although Dr. Chen's experience echoes that of other intellectuals, his penchant for the spotlight and theatrical nature cannot be considered typical of his generation. His relationship with contemporaries reflects another view of his place in modern Chinese history. During a time when non-Chinese ideologies became popular two opposing views on social reconstruction and national regeneration emerged. On one hand was the pragmatic, evolutionary method expounded by Hu Shi and later partially accepted by the Nationalist Party; and on the other, the Marxist revolutionary approach adopted by the Communist Party.[64]

Dr. Chen Renbing did what was expected of him as a member of the new generation who represented Chinese intellectual tradition. In the early period of his career, his motives were not questioned but rather it was he who assumed the task of questioning the motives of the government and making public his interpretation of events. From this prospective, it is possible to envision how he and his fellow intellectuals *raison d'etre* was horribly misunderstood and exploited by the Communist government in later years. Their fall from acceptance became their final disposition.

Endnotes

1. Chinese surnames precede familiar names, for example, Chen Renbing would be represented in an English language name order as Renbing Chen. This study uses the Pinyin system for transliterating Chinese names and terms. (Jiang Jieshi as Chiang Kai-shek; Sun Zhongshan as Sun Yat-sen). Chen Renbing's father was referred to as Chen Chong Gui, Ch'eng Chong Kwei or Marcus Ch'eng.

2.   John Foster was a colleague of Dr. Chen Renbing at Hua Zhong College, (also known as Central China University—formerly Boone University and Yale—in China and Welsley College) from 1936 to 1938.

3.   Author's note

4.   At that time one yuan was roughly equivalent to $.45 so that 57 Yuan would equal $25.75

5.   Jane A. Foster's Shanghai diary for Feb. 20, 1981 and John B. Foster's diary Feb. 19, 1981

6.   Letter to J.F. Ford from John B. Foster, October 26, 1992

7.   Chen was accompanied by his wife Liu Mingchin, a botanist, who also taught at Central China University.

8.   Interview with John Foster in Sarasota Florida 1993

10.   The medieval era lasted in China for more than two thousand years prolonged by peasant wars on a grand scale and frequent outbreaks made China lag behind the West in modern times while the medieval period in the West lasted only about one thousand years

11.   Staunchly ethnocentric, China was nearly destroyed by foreign weapons and treaties, beginning with its first contact with Portuguese sailors in 1514 and forty years later when shipwreck and storms forced permanent refuge. Permission to rent land and sell imported merchandise subsequently led other western powers to China. Spaniards came in 1575, Dutch in 1601, England in 1637, France in 1698 and finally the United States in 1784.

12.   Lin agreed with reformer Wei Yuan that intensified reform efforts needed to go beyond utility for the short run.

13.   Wei Yuan

14.   One example of economic trouble, was the dramatic shift in tea exports away from Guangzhou in southern China, north to Shanghai, one of the ports newly opened by terms of the Nanjing Treaty. In 1844 Guangzhou exported 69 million pounds of tea, dropping by more than half to only 27 million pounds in 1860. Conversely Shanghai had exported a mere 11 million pounds of tea in 1844, but increased to a whopping 53 million pounds in 1860.

15.   Hong's ideology came from a cousin who had lived in Hong Kong and was influenced by Swiss clergyman Reverend Theodore Hamburg and Englishman Reverend James Legge. Both Hamburg and Legge helped the cousin write a discourse of modernization the Taiping planned to implement. Hamburg even gave Hong's cousin money to go to Nanjing and then to Shanghai.

16.   Another futile attempt to modernize and westernize China was the short lived Reform Movement of 1898 when reformers Ceng Guofang and Li Hunchang urged hastening railway construction, adopting western arms , naval training, and establishing schools.

17.   Rong Hong was brought to the United States in 1847 by American missionary Reverend Samuel M. Brown.

18.   The 1902 code was replaced in 1903 with a new and modified set of regulations drawn up by an official commission

19.   With the Revolution of 1911-1912 came a change in the aim of school from developing loyalty to the emperor, reverence for Confucius, devotion to public welfare, admiration for the martial spirit and respect for industrial pursuits. Under the new regime, education became a means of cultivating virtuous or moral character, to instill into the minds of the people the right knowledge of liberty,

equality, and fraternity and, moral training. These lofty pursuits were supplemented by industrial and military education, and rounded out by aesthetic education.

20. In 1902 after returning from study in Japan, Zhang Taiyen, China's first sociologist, published "Sociology" in Shanghai, which advised China to follow Japan's example and use Western learning as a weapon to promulgate democratic ideas.

21. Hsu, Immanuel ((1975) 2nd ed. The Rise of Modern China. Oxford University Press: London. P. 495,496

22. Hsu, Immanuel ((1975) 2nd ed. The Rise of Modern China. Oxford University Press: London. P. 495,496

23. Qingha Weekly 1919

24. Cai Yuan Pei, Hanlin Academy member and returned student from Germany

25. Qinghua University English Supplement weekly of Thursday April 18, 1919

26. Qinghua Weekly 4/18/1919

27. Qingha Weekly 1919

28. Qinghua Weekly 1919

29. Qingha Weekly 1919

30. Qinghua Weekly 1919

31. Dr. Wang Zhen Ting

32. Qingha Weekly 1919

33. Ransom, George Twiss (1925) Science and Education in China: A Survey of the present status and a program for progressive improvement. Shanghai: The Commercial Press Ltd. p. 111

34. Hsu, Immanuel, 1975 The Rise of Modern China (2nd ed.) Oxford University Press: NY, p. 602

35. Hsu, Immanuel, 1975 The Rise of Modern China (2nd ed.) Oxford University Press: N.Y. p. 603

36. Fairbank, J.K. (1992) China: a new history, Belknap Press of Harvard University Press, Cambridge, MA., p. 53.

37. Weiss, Ruth F. (1985). Lu Xun : A Chinese Writer For All Times. New World Press: Beijing p.218 Mao's words were expunged from some versions of a book of Lu Xun's quotations and Weiss guessed that "one sentence in that speech offended the sensibilities of some ultra-Left people on the Committee for the Publication of Mao Zedong's Works right after liberation" (Liberation occurred in 1949)

38. Poteat, Gordon (1924) Home Letters from China. The Sunday School Board of the Southern Baptist Convention: NY."On conditions in China circa 1924" p. 143

39. Poteat, Gordon (1924) Home Letters from China. The Sunday School Board of the Southern Baptist Convention: NY."On conditions in China circa 1924" p. 143

40. Poteat, Gordon. (1940) Stand By For China. Friendship Press, NY. pp. 56, 57. Dr. Poteat cites Modern Trends in World Religions, edited by A. Eustace Haskell, University of Chicago Press p. 245 for the quotation by Dr. Hu Shi.

41. Earlier, Charles Sanders Peirce formulated and named pragmatism, a concept that predictions can be verified by future experience.

43.   See Index A in Keenan, B. 1977. *The Dewey Experiment in China: Educational Reform and Political Power in the Early Republic* Council on East Asian Studies Harvard University. Harvard University Press: Cambridge MA for an exhaustive list of all Dewey lecture dates and places, topics, translators and recorders.

44.   Keenan, B. 1977 *The Dewey Experiment in China: Educational Reform and Political Power in the Early Republic* Council on East Asian Studies Harvard University. Harvard University Press: Cambridge MA, p. 33

45.   Greider, J.B. Hu Shih and the Chinese Renaissance: Liberalism in the Chinese Revolution 1917-1937. Cambridge: Harvard University Press, 1970, p.23

46.   Keen, B. 1977 *The Dewey Experiment in China: Educational Reform and Political Power in the Early Republic* Council on East Asian Studies Harvard University. Harvard University Press: Cambridge MA

47.   Qinghua Weekly November 1919

48.   Qinghua Weekly November 1919

49.   On Thursday, November 20, 1919 at 3:00 in the Assembly Hall

50.   Qinghua Weekly November 1919

51.   Dewey's lectures at the National University in Peking included 16 on "social and Political Philosophy," 16 on "Philosophy of Education," 15 on "Ethics", 8 on "Types of Thinking" and 3 lectures each on "Three Philosophers of the Modern Period—William James, Henri Bergson, and Bertrand Russell", "Modern Trends in Education," and "Democratic Developments in America". The lectures were delivered in English, interpreted in Chinese as they were being given, and written down by recorders for use by the daily press and leading periodicals.

52.   Qinghua Weekly 1919

53.   Dewey, J. 1916 Democracy and Education. The Macmillan Company: NY

54.   Dr. Wang Zaoshi, classmate of *Luo Longji* at Qinghua and later at the University of Wisconsin was politically active and was also named a prominent rightist in the 1957 Anti-rightist campaign. Dr. Chen Renbing frequently mentions Dr. Wang in his biography.

55.   At the first Chinese Literary and Debate Society meeting *Luo Longji* presided.

56.   Qinghua Weekly Friday, November 14, 1919.

57.   "Human Rights and Political Engagement: *Luo Longji* in the 1930's" Fredric J. Spar article in "Jeans, R.B. (ed.) (1992). *Roads not taken: The Struggle of Opposition Parties in Twentieth Century China.* Westview Press: Boulder, CO, p. 62

58.   Spar in Jeans, R.B. p. 62

59.   Liang Shiqiu quoted in Greider, Jerome, 1970 Hu Shi and the Chinese Renaissance

60.   Coble, P.M. article *The National Salvation Association as a Political Party* in Jeans (ed.) Roads Not Taken, 1992, p. 138

61.   Jeans, R. B., (ed.). 1992. The Roads Not Taken: The Struggle of Opposition Parties in Twentieth-Century China. Westview Press: Boulder, CO, p. 23

62.   Chi, W.S. (1968). *Readings in Chinese communist documents: A manual for students of the Chinese language* (p. 189. Berkeley, CA: University of California Press.

63.   Spar, Fredric J. *In chapter Human Rights and Political Engagement: Luo Longji in the 1930s in Roads Not Taken*, Jeans, Roger B. (Ed.), (1992). Boulder, CO: Westview Press.

64.   Hsu, I. (1975). The rise of modern China (2nd ed.). New York: Oxford University Press (p. 615).

Chapter II: Chen Family Background

The Chen family saga begins around 1860. The rudiments of an immature Christianity[1] and the equality of men and women practiced within the ranks drew two women to become Taiping Rebellion[2] soldiers. When the Taiping Army of peasants and poor people were disbanded, these cadets drifted from Nanjing to Hubei and settled on the opposite banks of a river[3].

Both women married local men, and found themselves with child. The two brides arranged that if the offspring were of different sexes, they would join them in marriage. The precipitous issues, a girl surnamed Wang, who grew up to be a very sharp-witted and sharp-tongued lady, and a husky boy, Chen Chunghai became Chen Renbing's paternal great-grandparents.[4] Chen Chunghai learned the trade of barrel carpentry.[5] They had two sons, Chen Yuanching, Renbing's grandfather and Chen Yuanhe, his grand uncle whose clan settled outside the east gate of Wuchang city.

Chen's great-grandfather showed no leaning toward Christianity until he was about 80 years old. His grandfather joined the American Episcopalian mission church while he was young, and Chen Renbing's father joined the American Swedish Covenant Church congregation.

Chen Renbing's first and foremost influence was his father Chen Chonggui (1883-1963), also known as Marcus Chen[6] "perhaps the Chinese protégé of the Evangelical Covenant Church most well-known in both America and Sweden during the first half of this century."[7] We will see how Chen Renbing's emotional speeches were based on his father's techniques of the pulpit.

Marcus was born in Wuchang Hubei Province. Until around 1895, his childhood years were spent attending the Swedish American Church primary school whenever the family's economic situation allowed. Otherwise, Marcus was buying and selling steamed sweet potatoes with his brother Chung Fu. From 1896 to 1903, Marcus continued school and later graduated from 'Wesleyan College', a missionary school.He won the first prize in English in a tri-city contest. His knack for foreign languages landed him a prestigious and well-paying job in 1903 teaching English at the three 'yamens' (judicial authority offices). His family was aghast when he resigned his position to work in the Swedish Mission Church for a fraction of his former salary. In 1907, he married his first bride Chou Yenchung and she died the same year.[8]

In 1908, he married Mary Li (1882-1974). Chen's grandfather on his mother's side was a scholar, a herbal doctor of some fame and a lay preacher for the American Church Mission in Wuchang. He had four daughters and two sons. Mary Li was the eldest daughter. She attended the Methodist Girl's school.

Chen's aunt, China Democratic League leader, Li Wenyi (1902-   ) is his mother's youngest sister. She was married to Mr. Lo Yinong, famous Communist martyr who was executed for having led Shanghai Worker's Uprisings. Lo died in the April 12, 1927 "Massacre of Shanghai" ordered by Nationalist leader Jiang Jieshi.[9] Lo had worked closely with the late Premier Zhou Enlai.

Marcus, fluent in English and Swedish, began work in 1909[10] at the theological seminary of the American and Swedish Covenant at Jingzhou. In September 1909, Chen Renbing, John, was born and one month later accompanied his mother Mary to Jingzhou. From 1909 to 1925, Marcus and family stayed in Jingzhou and in 1912 witnessed both the birth of the Republic of China, and Joses their second son. Jonah was born and died in 1913 and in 1915 the fourth boy, Joel, arrived. In 1917, twin girls, Martha and Mary were welcomed to the family.[11]

From 1921 to 1922, Marcus and Mary traveled to the USA and Europe and Marcus stayed long enough in the States to become the first Chinese graduate of Wheaton College in Illinois.[12] In 1923, Marcus toured the camp of Feng Yuxiang[13] (a northern warlord known as "The Christian General") and son Joshua was born. The eighth and last child Merriam was born in 1924. In 1925, Marcus and family left Jingzhou for Zhangjiakou and Feng's Army headquarters where, for about 1 year, Marcus served as Chaplain General for Feng Yu Xiang's army. Chen Renbing wrote about Feng Yuxiang,

> A few years before 1923, my father was already well known in South and Central China cities as an evangelist speaker. He was a very welcome speaker at revival meetings, summer retreats, and so on even before he was ordained a Minister in 1923. He was invited by Marshall Feng to speak to his armies. My father's plain talks, human touches, simple but moving stories, won the heart of the generals and soldiers,

the common folks. There was no theological jargon, no threat of hell's perils. He just explained the Gospel and urged repentance so one could become a new man, be re-born with a Christian home life and Christian human relations.

Feng asked him to stay with his armies, but my father told Feng: 'I have to go back to my work as teacher at the small Jingzhou Seminary.' My father went back to his classes of theology at Jingzhou which he helped to found in 1907. In the summer of 1925, my father was told that he was no longer needed as a teacher and that 'you might do some research if you like to'. It was, of course, a polite way of saying 'you are needed no more'. My father smiled and said, 'Thank you, Marshall Feng has a standing offer to me, extended 3 years ago. I rejected that offer because I did not want to give up a small institution in favor of a big post'.

At the root of his dismissal was petty jealousy on the part of one or two of the Chinese faculty members, who were my fathers former students. So, my father wrote to Feng to say he was ready to accept the offer of 3 years earlier. A couple of months later, we were on our way to Zhangjiakou, where the headquarters of the Northwestern Army was located. (The picture of the Jingzhou school may be seen in my father's book *Echoes from China*.)[14]

Marcus Chen[15] was one of the indigenous preachers trained to lead an independent church in China envisioned by liberal Western missionaries like Dr. Gordon Poteat, who wrote in 1924,

We need not fear to say that our missionary task, as far as we foreigners are concerned, is largely an educational one: educational in church as well as in school. We shall doubtless always hold high our preaching services, but if we can organize Bible classes in small groups for the teaching of Christianity and get in contact with young people in the school room every day instead of only once a week, it seems to me that missionary work will prosper most. We must train the Chinese to be preachers, and so we too must preach, but one sees more than ever that the work of evangelization must be accomplished by men whose tongues have always used the Chinese language, and whose expressions are the idioms of the East rather than the West. China must be evangelized by the Chinese."[16]

In 1926, Marcus Chen and family left Zhangjiakou for Suiyuan, about 30 miles east of Baotou, to work in the China Inland Mission. About this time, Jiang Jieshi and conservative members split with radicals in the Nationalist party, purged Russian advisors and attacked military warlords and Chinese communists alike. Jiang set up a new government in Nanjing.

Feng Yuxiang, and a few other leaders cooperated with Jiang in a campaign against the Japanese. Bejing newspapers reported police were looking for a group of young Feng Yuxiang agents in Beijing. In this tense atmosphere the Chen family took refuge in a Swedish Church compound. The property included Swedish missionaries houses, a 1,000 seat church, an orphanage for girls, and a clinic. It was located outside the city of Suiyuan in Inner Mongolia.

Chen Renbing was 17 years old at this time and attended a mass meeting of unprecedented scale to propagate the popular political philosophy of Sun Zhongshan.[17] People everywhere were excited about Sun's concept, The Three Principles of the People. In China the notions of nationalism, democratic principles, and people's livelihood were new ideas. Chen Renbing attended the rally and recalled:

> The Division Commander of the area garrisons was there as well as Chamber of Commerce people, Rural Society leaders and, local bureaucrats. Students and teachers from three high schools and, of course, all the girls from the orphanage came out in a body to witness this historic rally.
>
> After the officials concluded their remarks the Magistrate announced that guest speeches were welcome from the audience. It was customary to include this invitation at public meetings. He repeated the call several times and no response came. Silence. Before the meeting, I did do some cramming on the Three Doctrines. Now, when the Magistrate solicited a "guest speech" for the fifth time, an unnamed urge drove me to join city dignitaries. In China, there is a saying, "the newly born oxen is not afraid of a tiger." I suppose that is what pushed me onto that high stage to speak to 15,000 strange faces.
>
> I said that the real spirit of 'Nationalism' was China for the Chinese, not for any imperialist. 'Democracy' simply means a China for the plain folk. Dr. Sun's 'livelihood' meant that 'we 400 million people should not only have enough rice to eat, but also good rice to eat'. The last quotation was verbatim from Sun's writings which I had just committed to memory.
>
> This marked my first venture at public speaking, the first time I obeyed an impulsive step into life beyond home and school. Right after the rally, excited girls from the orphanage told me how they appreciated my audacious little address, saying, they simply did not "get" what the Magistrate and Division Commander were saying and that to them only my remarks "made sense". I was really tickled by their encouragement.[18]

Chen Renbing discovered three things about himself that day. First, he was interested in politics, second he was good at public speaking and third, he enjoyed the attention he received. His penchant for public engagement was a blessing and curse.

Twin sisters, Mary and Martha were sent to Zhang Jia Kou Methodist Girl's School and Merriam and Joshua were too young for school. The Yu De School moved inland to Huhehaote, Inner Mongolia.[19] In 1925, his father accepted Marshall Feng's offer to become his Chaplain-General in Zhang Jia Kou. John (Renbing) Joses, and Joel[20] attended the Peking Yu De school[21] for military officers children south of the temple of heaven. They stayed only 1 year, yet, Chen wrote "it was a pivotal point in father's career as well as marking the start of the ways we children were to travel".[22]

> Feng[23] decided to promulgate Dr. Sun Yat Sen's "Three Principles of the People" and ordered enough reprints of abbreviated copies to distribute to his huge army. He told my father, "In my military life I've seen tens of thousands of my men and my enemies men cut down just like grass, without knowing what they died for. If we must fight more wars, they must be for some just cause. The men must know what they are fighting for."

> Two Shanghai college students were ostensibly Nationalists representatives but everyone knew they were Communists. One of them, Xuan Xiafu (1899-1938), lived next door and he introduced me to rudiments of Marxism and its application in China. He became a division commander of Communist anti-Japanese forces in the 1930's and wrote revolutionary poetry that eerily foretold of his end by a Nationalist executionist in Xian. He wrote:

> *People came out of their dreams step by step, As the voice of*
> *Revolution thundered on Remember this closely, dear comrades*
> *Freedom is bought with blood, nothing else.*

By summer's end 1926 the Yu De School went out of existence and Marshall Feng went to the Soviet Union.

Chen's father was in hiding for almost 1 year in this China Inland Mission and then sneaked through Shansi province to Shanghai to take up as Secretary of the Stewart Evangelical Fund. Joses and Renbing did self-study work in Suiyuan during 1925-26. In June 1928, Chen Renbing finished high school at the Peking Methodist Academy. His brother, Joses contracted scarlet fever and did not finish high school until June 1929 in Shanghai. Consequently, Joses was 1 year behind Renbing who majored in Sociology was graduated in 1932 from the University of Shanghai. Joses majored in Physics and transferred to Yenching University in Peking in his Junior year, graduating in 1933 with a BS in physics and later earned an MS in physics from Yenching.[24]

In 1927, Marcus went to Shanghai alone to become Secretary for the Stewart Fund and began the periodical *Evangelism* which he edited throughout his life. During winter the following year the family moved to Shanghai to join Marcus.

After their Suiyuan days, Chen's second brother Joel attended Peking Academy with him in the 1927-28 school year. When Renbing was in the University of Shanghai, Joel was in the University of Shanghai high school.

From 1927-28, Chen Renbing attended the Peking Methodist Academy to finish high school and during the latter year, Marcus joined the Chinese delegation to Jerusalem World Christian Conference. In 1930, Marcus Chen and family moved to Changsha to join the Bible Institute of Los Angeles (BIOLA) campus in China. The monthly journal *Evangelism*[25] also moved to Changsha. The Chen's lived there peacefully for 7 years until the 1937 Japanese invasion caused his family's move to Sichuan Province.[26]

CHEN RENBING'S SOJOURN TO THE UNITED STATES

Chen Renbing crossed the Pacific on board the S.S. President Taft on his way to study for a masters degree at the University of Southern California. He met and fell in love with Pearl Liu while aboard ship. Pearl was from Fuzhou province and graduated in Biology from Hua Nan Girl's School. She got a Botany MA from Syracuse University and returned to China where she worked as a high school principal and was returning to America to complete graduate school.

Chen witnessed the United States economy at its lowest point since the Depression of 1929 in his first year in Los Angeles, 1932. In September and October, Herbert Hoover and Franklin D. Roosevelt hotly contested the presidency. Chen recalled:

> During my first three months in the United States, I shared a house on Tremaine Avenue with an old Swedish couple, father's friends. That was before television and many nights we sat in front of the radio, listening to Roosevelt's fervent attacks and Hoover's desperate appeals for 4 more years. There was also a Socialist candidate, Mr. Norman Thomas. I know one family where father voted for Hoover, mother for Roosevelt and daughter for Thomas. I wrote an article about the election speeches and mailed it to *Life Weekly* in Shanghai, edited by Zhou Taofen.
>
> President Roosevelt's inspired inaugural speech, truly stimulated democratic idealism. Of the depths of crisis, he admitted, 'Values have shrunk to fantastic levels. The means of exchange are frozen in the currents of trade. The savings of many years in thousands of families are gone.' Bravely, President Roosevelt invoked faith and confidence, wishing American people to emulate their forefathers who 'believed and were not afraid.' What impressed me most was his historic assertion,

'The only thing we have to fear is fear itself'. Whenever I taught American history, I reminisced with pleasure that, together with tens of millions of Americans, I also was in that radio audience of January 1933.

A few weeks later a 'bank holiday' took place. I don't know if President Roosevelt set a precedent, but, suddenly one morning, all depositories and commercial banks closed their doors, not allowing withdrawals or checks to be cashed. Millionaires found themselves short of pocket money, managers stood at the side door of banks and only petty withdrawals to meet grocery and gasoline bills were granted. It wasn't too hard on me because I didn't have much of a bank balance anyhow. After a short time, arrangements were made and huge loads of greenbacks were shipped to major centers of the Federal Reserve Bank, in quantities enough for emergency cash demands. When Roosevelt lifted the limitations on withdrawals, there was no rush to the banks, confidence was restored. Roosevelt's mettle had been tested and survived the storm.

For a Chinese whose knowledge of capitalist economy came solely from text books, this was fresh and thought provoking indeed.[27]

Chen joined Pearl in Chicago that summer and he and Pearl worked at the World's Fair.[28] In the summer of 1933, they decided to pursue their doctorates at the University of Michigan at Ann Arbor where Pearl registered in the Botany Department and Chen joined the Sociology Department. They were married on July 20, 1934.

Pearl had her own laboratory in the Botany building for genetic and cytological studies of Genothera franciscana and was planting her own primroses in the University gardens south of the city. Shortly after their first daughter Ann was born, Pearl took her oral doctoral examination.

Chen felt that his American education was more complete with the experience of belonging to a fraternity, explaining that it fit in with the ancient Chinese tradition that 'All Men Are Brothers.'

In 1934, I was invited to join "Flip Flap", a Chinese fraternity for students attending American universities, founded in 1910 and named for a fashionable New York stage play. It was rather exceptional for a fraternity not to use Greek letters. Charter members included T.V. Soong, brother of Song Qiling and Song Meiling. We had five chapters and usually had annual reunions in New York or Chicago. For some time I chaired the local chapter. Our motto was "Fellowship and Service". To be sure, the initiation ceremonies, the novel experience, the secret ballot for admission, the sense of the mystic, half serious paddling, the absolute obedience requirement and the convivial group loyalty and sense of belonging all were gratifying and I treasure them always. In mid-July, 1934, I represented local Chinese Student Christian's at a national convention. There were about 300 Chinese students at Michigan at that time, quite a community by itself and Pearl automatically became a Flip Flap sister. She was also the founder and first chair of the Chinese girls students sorority, Sigma Sigma Phi.

When we "Flips" returned to China, we maintained national and local organizations, because membership was, of course, for life. When I returned to Wuhan in 1936, I found we had a over 10 fellows, including Mayor K.C. Wu. Our 1947 Shanghai chapter was strong, and we kept a nice size clubhouse at 16 Buck Road, employing 16 menservants. Our members including quite a number of outstanding lawyers, doctors, educators and business and religious leaders.[29]

In 1936, Mr. Toyohiko Kagawa, camouflaged as a Christian socialist, social reformer and consumer cooperative spokesman, spoke on the Ann Arbor campus to a 500-member Student's Christian Association about China's northern province, Manchuria. Kagawa explained the reason Japan occupied what they termed "Manchukuo" (site of the Japanese puppet government) was to prevent China from becoming "communized".

This assertion was too much for Chen and the others. Chen Renbing, immediately rose to challenge Kagawa and shouted, "Japan has no business in Chinese territory and to say 'prevent' this or that was nonsense. The Chinese government will never recognize it!"[30]

Beyond politics, Chen Renbing enriched his musical knowledge[31] and even tried his hand at acting[32] while in Michigan. On the strength of this experience Chen directed the 1942, 1943 and 1944, 240-voice choir rendition of the Messiah in Zhongqing and later at St. John's University in 1947 Shanghai.

Chen wrote, "In the years after returning to beloved China, I have always tried to be in the forefront of the amateur music movement, motivated by the revelations I had at Michigan. All my life, I could not be indifferent to the progress of music and drama, whether it was in wartime Zhongqing or among music hungry Overseas Chinese in Singapore or Kuala Lumpur or in post World War II Nanjing and Shanghai."[33] Chen's interest in music and theater was targeted for subsequent criticism in anti-intellectual campaigns after the 1949 communist victory over Jiang Jieshi's forces in a civil war and formation of Mao Zedong's socialist government in China.

CHEN'S RETURN TO CHINA

Chen Renbing, Pearl and Ann returned to China in September 1936.Chen began teaching sociology at Central China University in Wuchang where Pearl taught biology. But, because of the war, Pearl and Ann left Wuchang 1937 for Singapore, where Pearl taught in a high school.

On his way back to America on furlough in January 1940, John Foster took a boat from Rangoon to Hong Kong. John Foster wrote, "In Penang somehow I learned that Dr. Chen was in Penang with the Wuhan Songsters, the anti-Japanese song and dance troupe. I remember that he came out to my ship and we had a good visit about our mutual patriotic endeavors. My experience with the Chinese guerrillas made many friends for me in China and America."[34]

In August 1938, Chen led the Wuhan Songsters, a patriotic song and dance group on a fund-raising tour in Southeast Asia. The group left Canton on October 20, 1 day before the city fell to Japanese invaders. They performed in Macao and occupied Hong Kong, Singapore and Malaya until the summer of 1940. Chen still retained yellowed pages of a talk he had delivered.

> I seemed to take up speech making duties more than others, usually about every other night. Each night we offered 1 hour of choral singing, followed by a one-act play depicting the cruelty of Japanese militarists in China, detailing their atrocities and the valiant resistance of the Chinese. After singing and acting, we added another hour of patriotic speech making. Newspaper reporters tended to write about the talks as well as our songs and plays, so I had to write a new talk for each separate appearance. I remarked on our group's nature and purpose and gave a statement of our faith:

> Our songs and dramatic performance completed to audience applause and cheers, we drew the curtain and prepared the final panoramic tableau of slave-like figures silhouetted against forests, slopes and steps. The figures, dressed in tatters and clanking chains, bend their backs under the weight of labor, struggling up hills. A group of enemy soldiers with bayonets and whips flying, drive behind them. Then, the scene changes to show the same figures rising, throwing off burdens and breaking chains, setting siege to the bayonets and fighting with slave drivers while singing patriotic songs. Finally, the defeated enemies escape, falling. Fists raised, our gun toting figures singing lustily 'The Ultimate Victory is Ours.'[35]

In June 1940, Chen brought Pearl and Ann[36] back to China via Penang and Rangoon on the half finished Burma Road to Kunming. Chen worked for 1 month in Zhongqing at the International Broadcasting Station. Later, he joined the Ministry of Finance while at the same time was a professor of sociology at the National College for Social Education near Zhongqing.[37]

In 1946 the Ministry of Finance moved to Nanking, while the College for Social Education moved to Suzhou, with a branch school in Nanjing. Chen resigned from both the Finance Ministry and the College for Social Education to teach sociology at St. John's University in Shanghai 1947.

In Zhongqing in 1945 October, Chen joined the China Democratic League as an underground member. On May 22, he spoke to a mass meeting of 15,000 college students in Shanghai at an Anti-Jiang rally.

Chen Renbing considered Dr. Sun Zhongshan an idealist bred in the democratic traditions of England and America. He was inspired by Sun's political philosophy rich in patriotic sentiments toward China's problems of freedom, independence and social progress. In February 1947, at the beginning of the peak of China's civil war Chen began teaching required classes on Sun's Three Principles of the People at St. John's University.

According to Chen: "a whisper campaign began among more conservative American faculty members that I had turned my course into sort of a anti-Jiang Jieshi, anti-American forum. In the crucial year between July 1947 and June 1948, three major waves of student uprisings and urban demonstrations erupted as suppressive measures escalated."[38]

> I wrote a number of religious, social and political articles for *Tien Feng* magazine in the name of Christian ideals, social justice and equality, democracy and child welfare. My constant theme was that people's power was the source of all political strength. I also wrote a full analysis of Roosevelt's Four Freedoms in three long articles. In each piece, I wrote how people longed for the day when Chinese would find themselves free from fear of all sorts, specifically, fascist fear in which we took our every breath.

> I often perused recent U.S. publications at the public reading room of the American Consulate General in Hamilton House on Fuzhou Road. I made reading notes on Roosevelt, Truman, Dewey, Judd, Luce and produced articles on American democracy as well as foreign policy. *Harper's Magazine, The Atlantic, Life* and *The New Republic* provided food for thought and I wrote papers opposing U.S. military aid to Jiang Jieshi.[39]

> I drew the line between the friendship of the American people to China and the support of men like Judd and Luce for Nationalists die-hards. Just imagine, the source of my opposition articles was the public reading room of the U.S. government![40]

Against this background of political crisis, the Nationalists tightened their rule by arresting more democratic professors and progressive intellectuals. The *Outlook Weekly* which Chen and some friends founded in 1946 still managed to print powerful articles and Chen claimed it became an influential anti Jiang Jieshi organ. "Knowing the authorities could revoke our license at any minute, we wrote and wrote. There were demonstrations all over China, but the theme was always the same, opposition to Nationalists dictatorship."[41]

Chen considered political protests a second war front, side by side with the battlefield war of liberation. His religious articles advised against identifying the destiny of Chinese churches with that of interest groups or political set-ups.

Both Chen and Luo Longji criticized the Nationalists for hurriedly con-vening a National Congress and advancing a Constitution. Both groups gathered minus the participation or consent of either Chinese Communists or the China Democratic League. Public opinion was unfavorable to these despotic tendencies. Hu Shi was the chief nationalist representative at the Congress. Dr. Luo Longji, political activist since the 1920s and 1930s, and chief contributor to the *Crescent Monthly* edited by Dr. Hu Shi, opposed both the Nationalists and Communists for being undemocratic. Luo called them the "two evils, with the Nationalists being the lesser evil."[42] Dr. Luo "charged that American aid in support of one party against another, was contributing to the civil war in China."[43]

Landings of American marines in north China might complicate the country's internal political problems" 'The Americans,' he said, 'have always helped and we welcome their help in disarming the Japanese, but we hope it does not complicate the internal problem. There is a possibility that it might because Communist troops are stationed there. If the Central Government troops follow the Americans into big cities, there may be trou-ble.[44]

As spokesman for the China Democratic League, Luo commented on negotiations to end civil war and the equitable composition of a united front government between the Nationalists and Communists.[45] He met with Dr. John Leighton Stuart acquainting him with the "new state of sur-veillance over League members and expressed fear his arrest was imminent. "Democratic League leader Dr. Luo and other members in Nanjing were placed under house arrest."[46] This preceded a notice four months later that Luo Longji, a leader of the Left Wing Democratic League joined the Communists in boycotting the National Assembly because it was convened without Communist participation.[47]

Chen surmised if the peace pact between the Nationalists and Communists scheduled to be signed on midnight April 20, 1949 was not agreed upon, the Communists would certainly cross the Yangzi River and Nanjing would be liberated. Chen bought a ticket for Nanjing on the night of April 17, 1949 and slipped out of Shanghai on an almost empty train, avoiding spies who were closely watching routes to Canton and Hong Kong for progressive people.

On arrival in Nanjing, Chen immediately joined his Democratic League comrades in the work of welcoming the liberation army. In 1949, Chen was invited back to St. John's University to teach political science and became Dean of the Liberal Arts College. He stayed at this job until being transferred to Fudan University in 1952, when St. John's ceased to exist.

On Chen's visits to Tianjin, he found time to contact old friends[48] to request them to write contributing articles for the *Outlook Weekly*. He went for a short visit to Peking and came back to Shanghai quietly, secretly in January 1949. There Chen continued secret work for the Democratic League and the *Outlook Weekly*, until the *Weekly* was closed down by the Nationalists. In the spring of 1949, Chen was in danger of imminent arrest by the Nationalist spies. While civil war continued and just before Mao achieved victory over Jiang Jieshi's regime, Chen related,

> At these critical times, we democratic professors actively organized ourselves into discussion groups and had very interesting monthly dinners. We were known as the Union of Democratic College Professors and once, a few of us[49] complied with former Yenching University president and United States Ambassador John Leighton Stuart's request, and met at the 123 Tibet Road YMCA. Even though Ambassador Stuart's conclave with representative Shanghai professors was not mentioned in his memoirs, it was of some historic significance. Dr. Stuart started his talk by defending Jiang Jieshi's sincerity in trying to make his government honest and clean.

> Stuart said, 'Jiang knows there is corruption below. But, in the same proportion that strong public opinion against corruption exists, corruption will stop. You professors will be helping Jiang if you could help create a strong public opinion against corruption. It will come under control and a good government will ensue.' Among remarks I made in his face were, 'The Nationalists controls the newspapers and you can't forge public opinion through them; the Central News Agency is becoming the Central Lies Agency. Yesterday, it published a series of lies against a professor seated here tonight. As long as the United States extends aid to the Nationalists in its war against the Chinese people, like the recent loan of millions of bullets, the Chinese people will not forget. We have an elephant's memory! We Chinese accept American 'friendship', but, U.S. economic and war aid to Jiang Jieshi only makes matters worse!'

> To my remarks, Ambassador Stuart made no comment. Others spoke their minds frankly, in more or less the same vein. Stuart was trying to ask Chinese intellectuals NOT to doubt Jiang's sincerity. I hardly think he succeeded.[50]

Dr. Chen's year and a half at St. John's University was drawing to a close because his political activities and speeches were "too much for gentlemen like Dean of Arts, Professor James Pott to swallow." In the face of conflicts between conservatives and progressives on a national scale, peace in the laboratories and classrooms seemed as impossible as preventing patriotic students and faculty from joining the national sweep of anti-status quo currents.[51]

On August 27,1948, the birthday of Confucius, our ancient educator, a messenger knocked at my door and handed me a letter from Professor Pott which began,

"Dear Dr. Chen,

You are wanted by the police. They came for you yesterday and waited 2 hours." Pott went on to say that since the University already expressed it's wish that my employment not continue, would I please take myself off campus within 2 hours time. I didn't care a bit about James Pott, but I certainly minded quite a lot about what the secret police were doing this very moment. Were they still waiting outside the sole University gate? How could I escape?

Well, I figured I might as well take time to do a little packing. Clean shirts and a little cash in hand, I walked leisurely out the portal and no one stopped me. I walked to a well-informed friend's place and after some telephoning, he reported that no order for my immediate arrest had been issued.

However, to be on the safe side, from that day on I went into hiding. I remained a constant fugitive, yet I taught classes in the Social Sciences Department of the Shanghai Municipal Normal College, attended forums, visited friends, and frequented Nanjing Road teahouses. I changed my Shanghai address every two or three weeks, all the while scurrying for time to write contributions for anti-Jiang publications.

After I returned from Merriam's Tianjin deathbed (She died October 28, 1948), my Shanghai address was known only to liaison men in the China Democratic League. My cousin, Chen Rensheng belonged to the Shanghai underground Red Gang headed by Tiger Yang. He got me a couple of bogus identification cards showing my picture, but a false name. For some time I hid at Ren Sheng's home in a textile factory. His residence was comparatively safe from police searches. However, as far as I was concerned, perhaps no place on the continent was safe from spies.

As the last days of Nationalists rule approached, I was editing a weekly called *China Reconstructs*, on behalf of democratic businessman who planned to rent a room for me, when the necessity arose, in the U.S.-owned Broadway Mansions, an apartment complex. I never did stay and I was probably right not to trust that the Mansion agents would refuse to cooperate with Nationalists spies in a search for Communist suspects. Tensions ran high that half year before Shanghai's liberation. After lecturing at the Municipal College, some spying members of the Three Principles Youth Corps in my class would try to tail me. Obviously, they hadn't discovered my current residence, otherwise, I would have been arrested already.[52]

(The author regrets not asking Dr. Chen why the spies would not arrest him in public places.)

MARCUS CHEN IN POST-1949 CHINA

In 1948, after nearly four decades as a symbol of the success of Covenant Church missions, Marcus publicly supported the communist insurgency in China[53] in his capacity as well-known patriotic minister and teacher of religious philosophy. From 1950 to 1951, Marcus was one of the founders and elected as one of the six vice presidents of the Chinese Patriotic Association for Self Reliance, Self Support and Self Government of Christian Churches.[54] This "Three Self Patriotic Movement" was viewed by Marcus as an organization of Chinese Protestants who promoted Christian ideals as a way to reconstruct a better China. Critics accused it of helping the Communist government persecute the underground church.

Marcus spent from 1949 to 1950 in Zhongqing and from 1950 to 1954 Marcus and Mrs. Chen lived in Shanghai with eldest son Chen Renbing. In 1954, Marcus was selected to be officer of the National Salvation Organization, a Protestant movement. He and Mrs. Chen moved to Beijing and Marcus was invited to speak at the Beijing People's Consultative Conference. He often met with foreign religious leaders in the early years of the People's Republic.[55]

Chen Renbing wrote that "a thousand things commanded the daily attention of Zhou Enlai, but the affairs of the Christian churches in China seemed to be among one of his chief concerns."[56] Marcus was an ardent admirer of Premier Zhou. As an elected member of the National Committee of the People's Consultative Council in 1950, his speeches and reports on inspection trips to various provinces[57] concerned the people's courts and conditions of Christian churches. These reports were published in the People's Daily and attracted the attention of Zhou Enlai. Mao Zedong once shook Marcus' hand after a speech Marcus made at a Council convention.[58]

Two years later, Zhou Enlai asked Marcus to move and provided a three story furnished house in Beijing, formerly belonging to a bishop. The Chen's set up housekeeping, in accordance with Zhou's wish that Marcus receive Christian friends from all over the world.

Shanghai had always been the traditional center of Christian activities, so Zhou made arrangements enabling Mr. and Mrs. Chen to do work in Beijing, "winning and making friends for Chinese churches."[59]

In 1960 Premier Zhou invited Marcus to entertain Swedish statesman Dag Hammarskjold, Secretary General of the United Nations during his trip to China. Marcus spoke fluent Swedish and had been to Sweden. Naturally, he was glad to renew old friendships with some of

Hammarskjold's attaché's that had been colleagues in Hubei Province. Chen Renbing recalled,

> Zhou arrived 20 minutes early for Hammarskjold's farewell dinner. He spent the time chatting with my mother about Beijing life, and neighborhood unit organization and health care work. He asked whether mother provided the Swedish guests with foods they enjoyed in Hubei, nodding his approval when mother relayed how she asked the Beijing Hotel chef to prepare special dishes and had them sent to the guest's rooms. After that dinner, whenever Premier Zhou talked to my father, he would say, "How is Mrs. Chen? Remember to greet her for me." Mother died at age 92 in 1974. Throughout her life, she was always proud to relate Zhou's 20-minute chat with her.[60]

Ted Roberg said in *Marcus Ch'eng and the Covenant China Mission* (Ch'eng is another way to romanize 'Chen') that Chen believed missionary efforts in China must overcome identification with what Chinese considered unethical activities. "Marcus was treated as a 'trophy,' and spoken of as "the talented Marcus Ch'eng, loved by all of us, who won our hearts 6 years ago and now wins them again through his commitment to the well-being of missions and through his clear evangelical message". It is clear that Western missionaries thought of Chen as "their special link to China."[61]

Marcus wrote in *Echoes from China*, "During the last few years another difficulty has arisen. Some of our students who have studied in Europe and America have brought with them back to China atheism or other harmful 'isms'. They say and write that there is no God, no life after death. The worst is that they say Christianity is dying in the Western lands, that very few people believe in it and still less live up to it."[62]

Reverend Chen's most famous book was the *Daily Devotional Series*, a compilation of inspirational reading based on Bible passages. He wrote extensively on basic Bible theory and on how to be a good citizen and Christian. In all, he wrote over 40 books, including *Echoes From China*, an autobiography. Royalties from that slim volume provided the funds that initially sent Chen Renbing abroad to study. The book was looted away from Chen Renbing during the Cultural Revolution and through the kindness of a Swedish Covenant Church archivist in Chicago, a precious replacement copy was provided.

Roberg explains Marcus Chen's later political stances in light of his earlier religious life "Many thought it was impossible for a theologically conservative Christian to support a communist government. Some felt he had been duped; others wondered if he had either comprised or given up his faith.[63] In 1957, Marcus was branded a rightist and died March 8, 1963 in Beijing and in 1974, his wife died in Shanghai.

Chen Renbing wrote,

My father would not tolerate the corruption of the military lords, the Nationalist officials and in the same way he hated all deviation between words and action, never forgiving ingratitude to God and men. So, he was pained by the support tendered by American churches to the autocratic Nationalist regime, and was deeply hurt by the way the Communists repaid him for his hearty support of their causes. He appreciated Zhou Enlai's warm friendship for him, but he was deeply wounded by the way the younger "Christian" leaders and self appointed Church reformers cold-shouldered him after he was branded a rightist.[64]

Lost Siblings

In 1948, Chen's parents went to England and the United States for a preaching tour, leaving sister Merriam in his care. She was named for the biblical sister of Moses and attended the Central University at Nanjing majoring in fine arts and painting. In May of her sophomore year, she contracted tuberculosis, and in July, she was confined at Tianjin General Hospital.[65] Chen wrote, "Merriam died on October 28, 2 hours after I rushed by plane to her bedside. Her life could have been saved if penicillin in enough doses had been obtained."[66]

In later years, Joel went to study medicine at the Yale-in-China Medical College in Changsha. During the war in Zhongqing, he worked as a surgeon in a hospital west of Zhongqing, staying on to work until his death in 1968. After liberation this hospital was organized into the Seventh Military Medical University and Hospital of China. Joel became the head of the surgery department at both the university and the hospital. He also assumed the position as head of a research institute of surgery for national defense.

During the 10 chaotic years of the Cultural Revolution 1966-1976, three members of the Chen family met their deaths. In 1968, Joel was beaten to death, in 1974 Joses died by force.

Joel married Sheng Xiaoling, a nurse, and had three sons. Chen Renbing wrote of Joel:

> Joel was upright, industrious, kind-hearted and very sociable and the tallest of the four brothers. Emotionally Joel was close to me. We seemed to be of the same temperament. Joel graduated from the Yale-in China Medical College but had no chance to study abroad until 1948 when he was sent by the World Health Organization to go to America for advanced studies. He was sent to Boston University by the United Nations World Health Organization and studied medicine there for some time. When my parents visited the United States and Sweden in 1948-49 they saw Joel in Boston. His life in Zhongqing between 1949 and 1966 was a story of brilliant achievements. Joel was a popular doctor, an expert surgeon. He also served as a People's representative

in Zhongqing. In political affiliation he was a member of the "September Third Society", a democratic party named for the date of the Japanese surrender to China in 1945.

Joel never suspected that he should be beaten to death in 1968 by a couple of Red Guards, never dreamed that skillful hands that had operated on delicate cases should be tied behind his back and that he should be pushed on the ground and a few ruffians should stand on his chest so that seven ribs were broken.

In 1978, a grand memorial meeting was convened in Zhongqing to declare Joel a "revolutionary martyr."[67]

For many years, Joses was teaching assistant in Physics at Wuhan University, later moved to Loshan, Sichuan Province. Around 1946, he went to America to get his Ph.D. degree in Physics from the University of Southern California, Los Angeles, around 1950.

Joses was always good in math and natural sciences, but also wrote excellent Chinese. He leaned toward evangelism and fundamentalist gospel. He had plenty of evangelical tracts anyway. This way he avoided attracting the attention of inspections when he was sending all his scientific books home to China by mail because he specialized in atomic and nuclear physics.

After he came back to China he taught physics first in the University of Tianjin, and later until his death as the result of Red Guards cruelty (in 1974) at Nankai University. Joses died in August or September, while my mother died in March of 1974.

Joses played the violin and took part in amateur plays with me in 1930 and was very strict in moral conduct and self-discipline. He was an excellent scientist and science teacher. His wife, Wu Weiya also a Yenching graduate (history) was of the same type of extremely strict nature. They were very demanding.

In 1957, after I was capped a rightist, Joses took it seriously at face-value, not as a farce as many did, and cut off dealings with me.

As fate would have it, in the Cultural Revolution chaos, Joses was branded by the Red Guards as "a rightist who had escaped the net", and was ordered to cut grass to the amount of so many pounds by day, and write "confessions' of thousands of words by night.

Still frail from a youthful bout with scarlet fever, Joses could not have a chance to live. When Joses was working for his Ph.D. in the University of Southern California, he was dreaming that he would come to China and devote his life to atomic physics, which was very important for China. He did come back in 1951, and worked brilliantly for less than 20 years.

In 1966, the Cultural Revolution sponsored by Mao broke out and Joses never had the slightest idea that his career would end abruptly in 1974.[68] After the downfall of the gang of four, Joses, who had been a member of the China Society for the Promotion of Democracy, was officially declared a martyr of the revolution.[69]

Twin sisters, Martha and Mary went to high school in Changsha, and attended Wuhan University which moved to Lo Shan in Sichuan Province during the war. Martha majored in Chemistry while Mary majored in English literature. Mary died 40 days after her college graduation of illness.

Martha (Chen Meida) taught school and married a YMCA secretary. He was later ordained as a Methodist minister and, after liberation, served as minister at the International Church in Shanghai. He died of cancer in 1962. After 1950, Martha began to work as an engineer in a research institute in Shanghai testing materials. She has retired and has three sons. Martha characterized Chen's ideals and motivation:

> He wasn't a materialist, or a capitalist. He believed what was in his heart. He received Protestant influence. His ideals were based on the kingdom of heaven, not based in heaven but on earth. He supported democracy and peace, his principle was to treat everyone equally. He really respected American democracy, but also didn't fully agree with American democracy. He also didn't fully believe in communism. He just wanted everyone to be equal. He wasn't in favor of China being a strong country in control of smaller countries. If everyone could be equal and peaceful and have a lifestyle of freedom, the whole world could be in agreement.

> His principles also included Confucian ideals and other influences. In the end, he came up with his own ideas of what was right. Therefore, all his life he fought for the principles he believed in. When he lived in foreign countries, he hoped his motherland would be strong, become a leading country. He spent his whole life fighting for this. He gave up everything he owned; unfortunately, he ran into so much turmoil.[70]

ESTRANGEMENT WITH PEARL: POLITICAL AND PERSONAL

Professor Chen Ren Bing gives the impression of being either very pure or very naive. Estrangement in his marriage derived from the conflict between devotion to country and devotion to his wife and family.[71] This forced a cleavage to surface when Chen and Pearl were living in the Great China University in 1947. The inflation caused by the Nationalists civil war meant their combined salaries at Great China University and St. John's covered less than half a month's living expenses.

The political movements between 1950 and 1953 left Chen much to ponder on his marriage. This was true especially during the Thought Reform Movement when he had to make a clean account for all his thousand sentiments, "like pouring beans out of a bamboo tube". Chen wanted to have Pearl back, but began seriously to doubt how Pearl would fit in and adjust herself to such things for life in China.

Chen Meida remembers that Pearl was 6 years older than Chen, but "she was short and thin, you couldn't tell she was older than him." The Chen's "got along very well, but because of the situation there was no way out. He wanted to do China Democratic League work and she was afraid of war."[72]

Pearl was interested in her family's safety and conflicts arose because of Chen Renbing's commitment to political activism.

After Chen's 2-year stint leading the Wuhan Songsters, he took a job as Chinese and English language Transcript Director for the International Broadcasting Station in Zhongqing. The job paid $300 a month and was administered by the Nationalist Propaganda Ministry. Chen, Pearl, and Ann started from Kunming and reached Zhongqing after 6 days of risky and tiring travel. Unhappy with this position, Chen secured a job at the Ministry of Finance. Chen left Pearl and Ann in Wan Hsien with his parents and took a steamer upriver in September 1940.

Just when Chen began work, Pearl decided to leave China and return to teach in Singapore. She couldn't get work in Zhongqing, and it was tedious living in Wan Hsien. One of Chen's fraternity brothers,[73] helped her obtain a passport and she used all their savings to book air passage from Zhongqing to Rangoon for herself and Ann. Pearl was six months pregnant when she and Ann left in October 1940. When Chen went to the airport to see them off, they decided the new baby would be named either Frances or Francis.

On a steamship from Rangoon, with Penang in sight, their second daughter Frances was born prematurely. With careful feeding, she grew into a very healthy baby. In another year, the Pearl Harbor attack would separate Chen from his girls for the duration of the Pacific War. Chen spent 6 lonely years in Zhongqing without them.

While in Singapore, the Pacific War broke out. Pearl's school was closed and she and the girls suffered terrible privations. She took up private tutoring to survive. Victory came in 1945, and she came back to China in 1946 to join Chen. He writes, "How wonderful it would be if we had been able to pick up the broken threads and knit up our broken home life and live happily ever after."[74]

Postwar Nanjing living quarters were extremely scarce, but luckily the Chen family found a flat near the Ministry of Finance, on the second floor of a clinic. Chen stayed in Nanjing less than 1 year and Pearl's stay was even shorter. They set up housekeeping in the busy downtown area for no longer than a couple of months. Then, in December of 1946, Pearl accepted a job offered by the president of Da Xia University and left for Shanghai.

Pearl and Chen broke up again in May 1947. She had one room at Da Xia University and, Chen, being only a part-time professor, also was allotted only one room at St. John's. For a while they tried to manage, having the girl's attend school at St. John's primary school and eat lunch with Chen, while they all squeezed into the Da Xia University room at night. Their united income fell well below their minimum needs.

Pearl decided to return to Singapore for a few years. "Pearl tried to persuade me to go saying, 'There is not the slightest doubt you will get a good job.' I didn't doubt it either, but I could not consent to go with her. I only wished that she could stay in China."[75]

Their friend, now the mayor of Shanghai, helped Pearl get a passport again and she booked passage to depart from the same Shanghai wharf they had so happily returned to only 10 years before.

Pearl, Ann and Frances went to Singapore in May 1947. Pearl made a special effort to come to Fuzhou sometime in 1948 while Chen was a political fugitive in Shanghai. Between 1948 and the spring of 1949, Pearl taught at the Fuzhou Christian Union University Biology Department and intended to come and see Chen in Shanghai.

At the same time, Chen was expecting her to come back, and got a flat in the Shanghai Municipal Normal College dormitory. However, fearing the privations that 3 years in a surrounded city would surely bring about, Pearl went to the Fuzhou American Consulate, and, on the strength of the fact that she was the mother of American-born Ann, she obtained visas and tickets on the last boat leaving Fuzhou for Hong Kong. "Pearl informed me of her plans just five days before the boat sailed. With a heavy heart, I saw her and our two darling girls off. That was the last time I ever saw Pearl this side of eternity."[76]

The tragedy was, Pearl left Fuzhou for Singapore a few weeks before Fuzhou's liberation.[77] "Pearl and I would never see each other again. It came to my knowledge at a later stage, that Pearl went to the United States in 1956, while Ann preceded her mother by 2 years and graduated from the University of Michigan."[78]

In the first couple of years after liberation, when Chen traveled to Korea and was transferred to Fudan University, Pearl and the girls were in Singapore. She didn't know Chen was transferred to Fudan, and for some years after 1951, he did not know her whereabouts. "Sadly, there was a void of 2 or 3 years as far as our correspondence was concerned. I must say I bear the sole responsibility for the estrangement. Pearl never intended to stay very long in a foreign country."[79]

In 1956, a friend came back from West Germany and told Chen he heard Pearl was teaching somewhere in America.[80]

Chen went to Korea as a member of Chinese People's delegation to Comfort the People's volunteers to Korea 1952. He was vice president and general secretary of the Shanghai Committee of the China Democratic League 1956 to 1957 and Associate Chief Secretary to the People's Political Consultative Council of Shanghai from 1956 to 1957.

It was at this point in Chen Renbing's life that he finally made up his mind to ask for a divorce from Pearl. The Shanghai Court requested her address, but Chen did not know it. He gave the Court the name of a mutual friend who might have Pearl's address, but Chen did not know where the friend lived either.

The Court had its way of finding the friend, and, had her forward the request to somewhere in America. Unfortunately, after the initial forwarding of Chen's request for divorce, the Court misplaced the friend's address. Later, when Chen tried to contact the friend, he was told the friend had moved to Wuhan and was deceased. The thread with Pearl was broken.

In 1958, the Shanghai People's Civil Court received Pearl's handwritten agreement, and officially granted the divorce. Six years later, in January 1964, Chen married Miss Chen Yuinhui, a maternity doctor in Shanghai. In November the same year, their son Chen Jiaxin was born. Pearl did not know Chen's address until 1970 when she found it out through the Chinese Embassy in Italy. She wrote to him immediately.

> Chen Meida relates the sequence of events that transpired when Pearl returned:

> My brother was very happy. On one side, she came to China to teach, on the other hand she came to visit. No one knew if, in fact, she was coming as a foreign expert, so, eventually she came on a family visa. Before 1973 she wrote a letter that she was applying for an immediate return. My brother wrote and told her, first enter Guangzhou and then go to Shanghai. After coming to Shanghai, my brother planned to take her to Hangzhou sightseeing before she went back.

> Pearl never received his letter, as she already left the place. She wrote a letter telling my brother which day she would arrive in Guangzhou, later on, she went from Guangzhou to Beijing. In the time it took for him to get the letter, there wasn't enough time. He sent a letter to the Guangzhou hotel, asking the hotel to pass the letter on to her.

> My sister-in-law didn't know the situation in China, she wrote a letter and wanted my brother to go there to meet her and afterwards, go together to Beijing. At that time my brother still was a rightist. He couldn't move around freely, also he had no money to go to Guangzhou. In addition, he didn't know her flight number, he didn't

know anything! He had no way to meet her. Therefore, the best he could do was write a letter to the hotel, ask the travel service to give it to her. In the end, it didn't reach her.

That letter told her not to go to Beijing, also told her that my brother could not come down to meet her, and asked her to come to Shanghai. This way, they could get together. In the end, she never got that letter, and she herself went to Beijing. She stayed in Beijing 10 days and later went to Guangzhou and stayed a month and then went back to America. My brother also tried to find her because she said she would go to Guangzhou on July 10.

Then at the middle of July until early August she should have come to Shanghai. My brother also contacted big hotels in Shanghai, requesting that if such a person came, they would contact him. There was no news in Shanghai. Later on he tried to contact her, but got no news.

After she left, my little brother at the Beijing Fangdian found out she had stayed there for 10 days. In those 10 days, she did not mention she was looking for anyone. Afterwards, my brother wrote her a letter, but after she returned to America she was very angry, didn't write any letters to my brother, even though he wrote to explain things to her. Ultimately, I don't know if she got that letter. She wrote and said, you needn't send me any more letters. Because we already have no relations. Later on, about a year later, she contracted lung cancer and died in 1974.[81]

THE ANTI-RIGHTIST MOVEMENT

Chen lost his position in the China Democratic League during the 1957 Anti-Rightist Campaign recriminations against perceived attacks on the Communist party. In 1956 Mao Zedong invited intellectuals to offer suggestions on how to rectify party practices and later conceded that the offer to "Let One Hundred Flowers Bloom, Let One Hundred Schools of Thought Contend" was a trap meant to ensnare those who clung to bourgeois thinking.

"Rightists" were punished by the degree of their alleged transgression. A mild punishment would be demotion and cut in salary, severe punishment meant incarceration for re-education or banishment and ostracism to the hinterlands for 20 or more years.

Chen Ren Bing was personally criticized by Mao Zedong and named the "biggest southern rightist" for comments he made about the film industry. During the summer of 1957, Shanghai and Beijing newspapers ran a massive campaign of bold headlines and caricatures of Chen, with accompanying articles that caustically eroded his reputation.

Chen Renbing's loyalty to the young Marxist government and his naive perception of a scholarly obligation to voice dissent cost him his marriage. Chen was unable to criticize successfully in the name of Communist party rectification and unable to defend himself when denounced. Mao Zedong personally singled Chen out in 1957 and again in 1965 before the beginning of the Cultural Revolution when Chen was labeled a playboy who "fanned the flames of capitalism".

Ostracized from 1957 and throughout the Cultural Revolution, at the time of his death he remained the last Rightist denied restored status and rights resulting from being accused of anti-government crimes, in other words, a rectified 'rightist' who had not been wrongly capped.

Madame Li Wenyi[82] described the situation that led to events in 1957.

> In 1957, the Chinese Communist Party asked people outside the Party, and all Chinese people to criticize the failings and mistakes of the Communist Party. The Party wanted to develop democracy and correct common Party practices to manage the whole country better.
>
> However, in 1956, anti-revolutionary incidents in Hungary and Poland influenced China. Some people did not approve of party's leaders going against socialism. Criticisms were made of those in Eastern Europe who engaged students, peasants and workers to cause trouble and create disturbance against the communist party.
>
> There were two different contradictions, first among workers, peasants and students and second, among a few people who engaged them. Some bad eggs felt the contradictions stemmed from a different rationale. But because these different groups crossed, it was quite difficult to separate them.[83]

The Mao Zedong slogan in his February 27, 1957 article on internal contradictions among the people, "Let A Hundred Flowers Bloom, Let A Hundred Schools of Thought Contend" was meant to encourage thinking and expression of intellectuals outside the Party on artistic and scientific matters.

Mao brought out his double hundred call with his contention that the democratic parties and the Communist Party should co-exist for a long time, and should practice mutual overseeing. In 1956 Mao invited intellectuals to offer suggestions on how to help rectify the Communist party.

During the climax of the Anti-Rightist Movement, however, those branded "rightists" were accused of taking advantage to mount attacks against the Party.

In 1957, thousands of intellectuals were punished by the degree of their alleged transgression. The punishment for being "capped" a "Rightist", aside from the obvious humiliation, public criticism and disgrace, was meted out in six different degrees, according to the perceived severity of one's "crime". When a professional position was revoked, one's salary was reduced to a fraction of the original amount. From most severe to weakest, the prescribed chastisements were:

1.Reform by labor (sometimes in a distant location), professional position canceled.

2.Labor as you can (for older people), professional position canceled.

3.Living subsidy or "salary" but much less than usual, professional position canceled.

4.Discharge from professorship, title is deprived, salary lowered two scales.

5.Demotion in salary one scale, retain professorship intact.

6.Titled "rightist" but with no material punishment.

Chen Renbing writes, "As far as the general public was aware, the 1957 internal rectification of the Party did not seem to have accomplished much. On the contrary, it's by-product, the Anti-Rightist Campaign yielded much. The number of "rightists" capped during 1957-58 (mainly in 1957) was variously estimated at from half a million to 600,000 persons. No one knows for sure. In my family, my father, my kid brother Joshua and myself were all branded. Had my wife Pearl been in China that fatal year, the probability that she would have been rounded up was pretty high too. Approximately one third of the Central Committee of the China Democratic League were labeled "rightist." So were about one fifth of China Democratic League members."[84]

What actually took place was, hundreds of thousands of intellectuals were looked upon as "enemies of the people", and their writings and speeches were treated like "venom of oxen devils and serpent spirits".

Mao wrote an editorial for the People's Daily accusing intellectuals of "cherishing a hatred for having been robbed of their country". This was, of course, absurd, because the victims of the Movement were, Chen writes, "without exception, well known, fervent Chinese patriots of long standing".

Chen explained that according to Mao, "open traps" and not "hidden traps" were laid for the "rightists" during the month from May 8 to June 7, 1957 in national newspapers. He merely waited for "rightists" to say all they wanted to. Then, they were clamped down upon in a wave of leftist criticism.[85] Commenting on her nephew's predicament, Li wrote, "Chen Renbing, at that time was the Vice-Director of the China Democratic League and professor at Fudan University. I don't know what he said, but he was the biggest rightist in Shanghai. The government didn't let him teach and he was forced to go to the countryside to work at reform through labor. In that period of time it was very hard for him."[86]

Was Professor Chen too naive during the Anti-Rightist Movement? He was, after all, quite willing to admit his shortcomings when many other intellectuals resisted in giving in and admit their thinking was wrong? Li Wenyi wrote,

> As for my point of view, I think Renbing was quite open-minded, open-hearted and outspoken, yet he wore his heart on his sleeve. If he had the opportunity he often spoke directly without thinking, so often other people will have a false impression of him. But I deeply feel that he always loved our country and he knew only the Communist party can save China and socialism is the only way to get a peaceful life. He never was against socialism and the Communist party. He definitely was not an anti-revolutionary.[87]

Dr. Chen had three younger brothers and three younger sisters. His father and youngest brother were also capped in 1957, and, by 1962 were fully "corrected" and "rectified". "The fact that father was so hurt by the Party did not stop him from his friendly devotion to it as shown in his poem to his son who was also deeply wronged by the party."[88]

One of the saddest consequences of the Anti-Rightist Movement for Dr. Chen was the deterioration of relations with one other brother, Joses. "In 1957, after I was capped a rightist, Joses cut off dealings with me."

After Chen Renbing's "rightist" cap was removed he was allowed to offer courses in the History of England and the United States at Fudan University between the years 1961 and 1963.

THE CULTURAL REVOLUTION

Shortly after his son was born in November 1964, Chen was dragged into another political quagmire when "someone high up in Shanghai concocted a new case"[89] against him and consequently Chen received yet another degradation in salary and a demotion.

On an April 1965 morning meeting of the entire faculty and staff of the History Department it was announced that Chen was fired from his teaching job he had held since 1953. Chen was transferred to the Fudan University Carpenter Shop as a common worker.

When the Cultural Revolution came like a bolt from the sky, Chen had already experienced the shock of being unceremoniously removed from a long gowned job (Chinese equivalent of a white collar worker) to that of manual laborer. "I comforted myself with the thought that maybe it was not so bad after all. Was not my grandfather a carpenter in Wuchang?"[90]

In 1966, when the Cultural Revolution started, Chen was learning to operate semi-mechanical and electric saws and planes. In other words, he was no longer a "counter-revolutionary scientific authority" teaching in a university, but a mere coolie.

That made some difference, because, already deprived of my status, the party could not make Chen a "Black Example" peddler of "reactionary capitalist learning". He did not have to make detailed "anatomical analysis" of his "reactionary systems of thought and learning". Chen said, "What was there to analyze about a carpenter's sporadic thinking?"[91]

From descriptions given by Chen and others, to have one's own "system of counter-revolutionary thoughts criticized" was no light matter. Big character posters containing more than a 100,000 words were pasted in front of your door, followed by "struggle meetings" in which a thousand red guards shouted at you, made you kneel down, twisted your arms behind your back until they nearly broke, boxed your ears, slapped your face, all the while spitting and swearing at you and beating you in front of a crowd.

Dr. Chen wrote of many professors who received doses like these at the initial stage of the so-called Cultural Revolution.

> The famous Chinese historian Li Pingxin of East China Normal University lived in the apartment above mine. He also had been wanted by Jiang Jieshi's spies before liberation. One day, large character posters attacking him as a "counter-revolutionary authority of capitalist learning" appeared by the dozen and covered all the available wall space in the courtyard behind our apartment house.

> I don't know what happened to him at the East China Normal University, but I'm sure he got the beatings while he knelt, while they spit at him, twisted his arms and slapped at his face. I suppose he couldn't take it. The afternoon of the second day, Professor Li came home and sent his maid servant out for some errand, turned on the gas and committed suicide. He was divorced and lived alone, except for the servant. His suicide in the first week of anarchy was only one of many similar cases which followed in the course of 10 years.[92]

In the first days of June 1966, Chen was naïve. What happened to his neighbor Professor Li, did not constitute a warning to him. When the red guards looted and ransacked the empty apartment one floor above Chen, he still took no signal as he thought they might have a reason for being ransacked. The apartment was the home of an attorney for the Municipal Court in the days of the British Settlement half a century ago, who was not in China.

However, the very next night, August 31,1966, the red guards descended on Chen's apartment.

> There were 40 of them, kids from a normal school, headed by a sort of teacher. In view of what happened to our upstairs neighbor, my wife was just leaving our apartment. She was going to her relatives nearby to deposit a few gold trinkets she carried in her handbag. She was

> stopped on the steps outside our door and ordered back into the apartment.
>
> The ransacking was through. It lasted from seven o'clock P.M. until seven o'clock A.M. The 40 pairs of hands were mighty busy, opening every book and looking into the contents of every notebook. I had a trunk full of class room lecture notes and thousands of classified cards of reading and research materials accumulated over 30 years of college teaching. The red guards loosened each bundle and poured over the contents. No wonder it took a whole night to do it.
>
> In the meantime, they carted away my books, Chinese and English, new and old, large bundles of them in pedicabs. They stole carts full of my stuff. My wife and I were ordered to stay in another room and not allowed to know what was happening to our belongings.
>
> I don't know just what were the books, maps, documents and periodicals they took away from me. It was 17 years ago. I never saw those books again. My heart ached at some of the rare books and unrecoverable documents they took away. The mimeographed copy of my father's autobiography was looted away. It was the only copy existing, because other copies were long ago lost. My BA diploma issued by the University of Shanghai, MA from the University of Southern California were gone.
>
> My Doctor of Philosophy sheepskin. wrinkled and rolled into a ball, was thrown into a corner. Such a precious thing, one would almost think the red guard kids mighty considerate in sparing that testament to the highest degree. The fact was, they never did know what these things were. Otherwise, I would not have a single piece left. Gone was my MA thesis on Dr. Sun Zhongshan and my Ph.D. thesis on Population Balance, which represented 3 years of sweaty work.
>
> In desperation, I wrote my alma mater 8 years later of my loss, not going into the intricacies, mind you. I was extremely moved and grateful when they sent me a replica of my dissertation, cloth bound and gold-lettered, free of charge.[93]

Chen poignantly recalled that the willful act of destruction by agents of a so-called Cultural Revolution was salvaged by the good will of a foreign university.

When the red guards finally left that morning of September 1, they ordered Chen to write a full confession of his "rightist crimes" to be submitted that evening. Although he did not sleep the night before, he went to the Fudan University carpentry shop to ask leave for the day.

However, the young ruffians did not show up the next few nights. The entire group of 40 did come again on September 18 at seven o'clock P.M.

From evening until morning the red guards spent another night ransacking things they had not taken away the first time. Toward the morning of September 19, they piled up papers and books and threatened, "We will come for these things tonight, in the meantime, we will seal up your bedroom". Chen wrote,

> We hastily took out a few things we needed for our 2-year old son. The red guards pasted a few strips of paper over the doors and signed their names on them. In old China, a mandarin would paste a slip over your door and put a red seal over it. The plain folk could only tear down the seal under pain of death.

> This time, the red guards did not come that night. In fact, they didn't show up again for several months. When September turned into October and October into November, the winter weather set in and we only had our summer clothes. We did not know where the red guards were, and for the life of us, we did not dare touch the sealing papers.

> Our winter clothes were stored in the bedroom. We had only to raise our hands two feet high and tear down the darn things, and open the door. My sister Martha loaned me a blue silk cotton padded coat to wear under my overcoat, because all of my cotton padded clothing was locked in that sealed room. My wife also borrowed a red silk cotton padded garment from Martha to resist the winter weather.

> In late November, the weather got colder and colder. Between our bathroom and the sealed bedroom there was an opening for ventilation, a small transom 10 feet high off the floor and one foot below the ceiling, just big enough for a trim body to wriggle through.

> My wife got desperate one night about midnight. We shut off all the lights and she managed to climb through the window with trembling hands and a pounding heart. We committed the crime of burglarizing our own bedroom and were scared to death while going about it. We retrieved heavy cotton underwear for the whole family and all our woolen things for winter. That thievery saved us from getting sick from the cold.[94]

The red guards did not show up to unseal the Chen's bedroom until almost the end of December. It is difficult to imagine how many other rooms red guards had sealed in the meantime. Chen explained that they never bothered to explain why the "next" day turned out to be several months later.

Instead, when they did return to Chen's apartment they told him and his wife to clear all of their things out of the parlor and dining room. They announced, "We are going to use them as offices of the headquarters of our regiment. Hereafter, your whole family will live in your bedroom." For almost a year, the red guards commandeered the largest room in Chen's apartment.

This did not prevent other red guard detachments from further plundering and looting Chen's belongings and books. All told, the Chen's were ransacked nine times in 1966.

There was a saying often quoted by Mao Zedong that "there are 1,000 years of fortune if you could be certain of things but 3 days before they took place"

Eventually, Chen was forced to give up the apartment he lived in for 15 years and move to a slum area. Before that, however, Chen was virtually put under arrest, called "segregated examination", for four months during the Spring of 1968 by the Chou Fan Pai (The Rebels) who were law unto themselves.

That sort of imprisonment, without any legal procedure was for an indefinite period. Some were held half a year, others 3 or 4 years. On April 29, 1968, Chen was shouted at and bombarded with questions at a Fudan University meeting. Then, the rebels closed the meeting, packed him in a car and drove Chen to his apartment, ordering him to pack bedding and a few pieces of clothing. They returned Chen to Fudan University to his prison, at first an unused garage with no windows.

> Three of us, myself, a chauffeur and a taxi driver, were housed in this temporary jail. After a few days, we were transferred to the ground floor of a dormitory[95] that used to be for Vietnamese students. All the windows were barred, a locked door to the corridor was added. A few Rebel Group members were on guard duty day and night. Each time we went to the washroom, we had to ask the guard to unlock the door which communicated to the outside world.

> At night, the overhead bulb was never extinguished, as prison rules all over the world seem to demand. The worst part of the business was, we were not allowed to take a nap during the noon hour, not a wink. Under the pretense of reading Mao Zedong's Quotations, at the only desk in the room, we might feign study in order to steal a bit of repose. Anytime, day or night, during those four months, we were apt to be called away for interrogations. Actually "trials" were more likely held at night in some Lecture or Science Hall classroom or office, usually high up on the fourth or fifth floor where it was quieter.

> We heard midnight howling and cries of pain from those rooms in the depth of night, for violence was freely used. During my interrogation sessions, I often saw a guy standing behind me holding a section of rubber hose. Luckily, they never used it on my person, nor was I ever whipped, not an infrequent occurrence in those days. Maybe they took pity on me because of my age, I was 59 in 1968. But, no, I've known cases of 70-year old people being whipped and beaten. My age didn't help on another occasion I received 50 blows on my face, administered

by husky cooks from the University student's kitchen. For a week, I couldn't open my mouth.[96]

Chen was ordered to kneel on the cement floor of the Lecture Halls for hours at a time during all the inquiry sessions. It happened that his knee cap had an abnormally protruding bone, so kneeling was more painful. He went through this ordeal for countless nights. When he began this "segregated examination" forced custody, it was April and he wore heavy cotton undergarments. Chen said, "Those padded underwear were a godsend on many a long kneeling session. When the weather got warmer, I kept those useful heavy pants on. Around June and July, I was sweating from the heat, but I still kept wearing those precious underwear."[97]

Chen was released from "segregation" in late July, restored his freedom and sent home. He resumed his job at the Carpenter Shop. As a result of the "Examination", Chen was formally branded a "counter-revolutionary element" accused of having opposed the Great Leader Lin Biao with disrespectful language. Slander against Lin was a serious crime. Had Lin Biao[98] not subsequently exploded himself, Chen would likely found himself in an inextricable situation and summarily shot for my "crime".

Not long after Chen was released, his apartment was taken over by Fudan University "rebel gang" chieftains, Chang Yunfa and Liang Yinbao. They were in charge of Chen's interrogations and commanded Chen to hand over his house rent receipt book issued by the Housing Bureau of Shanghai. This book was equivalent to government permission to reside in an appointed dwelling.

After getting hold of that document, Chang and Liang went to the government housing bureau and simply said, "We have use for this apartment. As for Chen Renbing, we have another place for him to live." Because the rent for Chen's apartment was too high for them, they asked the Bureau to let them have a cheaper apartment at nearby 170 Chang Lo Road. Liang Yinbao moved his family in immediately.

Chen was forced to move because Liang obtained a new residence on the strength of Chen's apartment. One Saturday morning, Chen was first ordered to read a few quotations from Chairman Mao's little red book. That done, the rebels issued a command that his family move out. Chen was ordered to go to a certain place to look over the dwelling in the company of a certain gentleman, and made to move there within 2 or 3 days. Chen recalled:

> I was led to a slum area in northwest Shanghai, just outside where the St. John's University back gate used to be. Our new abode consisted of two rooms, eight square meters each. Initially, my wife refused to change addresses, so I delayed moving for a week or so. Another meeting was called and I was made to bend my body low and bow my head, while suffering humiliations and stern abuse for "daring to resist the order to vacate, according to a command issued by the

Revolutionaries". I sold more than half of my furniture, because my old place was more than 70 square meters.

Afterwards, I found we moved into the slum rooms recently vacated by the estimable Rebel Liang Yinbao! We had electric lights, but there was no flush toilet, no gas and no running water. We had to line up out in the lane for water from a common spigot. Here, we spent our next 10 years, thanks to the enthusiasm of Honorable Rebel Liang to "reform" me, an ex-"rightist."

In those unprecedented days of rebelling, it was the lot of intellectuals, most of them called "oxen devils and serpent spirits," to obey explicitly all commands from Rebels and Red Guards. No questions asked.

The first day I was regimented into the "Labor Squads of Oxen Gods and Serpent Spirits", the men of our entire team were ordered to have our heads shaved clean during lunch hour. We did and, when I went home that day, my toddler son didn't recognize me and cried with fright.

This summed up the entire 10 years. You did what you were commanded. You could not choose the house you lived in. You were ordered to shave your head and there was no shrinking from it. One lady doctor in our team was besieged by Rebels who shaved half the hair off her pretty head. She resisted desperately, but to no avail. The Cultural Revolutionists took pride and joy in robbing personal rights and dignity to the last shred, and they leered over their triumphs.

They routinely ordered people to climb on all fours, up and down five flights of stairs during "struggle meetings." I have been put through some of this chastisement, but fortunately at levels closer to the ground floors.[99]

In an April 8, 1988 letter, Dr. Chen wrote, "Politically I am still an "unrectified' 1957 rightist." That is, Chen was restored to his former position at the university but he was one of five people who were determined to not have been wrongly labeled a rightist. Lin Wen Yi confirmed that " Chen Renbing didn't get rectified. But, he recovered his position at Fudan University.

The China Democratic League and Party gave him some recognition late in his life. In 1990 the Party gave him an eightieth birthday party, and after his death a memorial".[100]

After the Cultural Revolution ended in 1976, many secrets of the Party were exposed. After the fall of the "Gang of Four", secret files maintained on all intellectuals who came back from abroad, revealed that they had been shadowed by the Public Security Bureau since they returned.

Many were labeled as foreign spies. These documents consisting of police reports and "confessions" people had written. The secret dossiers were made public, and, were returned to their owners after the downfall of the Gang of Four. Intellectuals discovered that the government had demanded too much of them.

Information leaked that many intellectuals who had been "branded" during the Anti-Rightist Movement in 1957, were not targeted necessarily by what they said or did not say, but "capped" to fill a quota of "rightists" determined to exist in their respective departments. Chen Renbing wrote:

> Looking back over the years, my father and his four boys were drafted by democratic parties in a very natural way. Love our country, love your people, pick a party to join and devote your efforts. Three of us joined the China Democratic League. Joel joined the September Third Society which was mainly for scientists. Joses joined the Society for the Advancement of Democracy. Father felt it was necessary to both serve God and actively work for China's democratic process.

> I cannot help recall again and again the fate in 1968, of how my third brother, Dr. Joel Chen, died. After he was trampled to death, they found six broken ribs, two penetrating his lungs. The Gang of Four had taken us back to a barbaric age.

> When Joel finally met his death, I don't know what he was thinking as red guards attacked him like a gang of mad dogs. What was his dying wish? In that split second, did he wish China of the future could be more democratic, more rational and humane?

> Another family victim was my second brother Joses, Renlieh Chen, Ph.D. in Nuclear Physics from the University of Southern California. At the height of the disaster, Joses was branded "a rightist who slipped through the dragnet" and was put through the routine of interrogation, criticism and forced to write endless "confessions", perform forced labor, with heaping doses of humiliation and bodily molestation thrown in.

> Joses suffered from critical heart disease, left over from a childhood bout of scarlet fever. He was ordered to hand in a fixed amount of labor per diem, and, at night he was forced to sit up for hours of "rightist confession" writing. At the end, he could not elude the drag- net of death. That was on September 14, 1974.

> While in Beijing, I lined up with hundreds of people to walk slowly around the embalmed body of Mao Zedong, hero of the Chinese Revolution and creator of the Cultural Revolution. Approaching his body, I did not cry.

> My tears dried long ago, when my brothers were murdered. It is hard
> to relate just how I managed to survive the stormy days and nights of
> those 10 years. Nevertheless, seeing Tian An Men Square again gave
> me renewed faith in the latent power of the Chinese people.[101]

For Chen Renbing, it was heart-rendering to think of the long years he was
compelled to give up teaching and research. In his spare time, he managed
to translate biographies of 20 world famous scientists from English into
Chinese as well as the History of the English Revolution 1640. He did part
of a translation of Toynbee's, *The World In March 1939*. He also compiled
a book of readings entitled Selected Readings (in English) for Students of
World History, Volumes 1 and 2.

Dr. Chen used this book for a course in World History he taught at
Fudan in 1961 and 1962, then, after a long interval, from 1980-84. About
10 years before his death, he wrote, "If I can, I want to make up for lost
time by writing a simple text on Urban Sociology, one of my favorite subjects. I also want to write something about Political Sociology because long
ago, I found myself entangled in China's political arena, whether I wished
it or not."[102]

CHEN'S CONTEMPORARIES

Intellectuals of Chen Renbing's generation were raised in a changing world.
Many returned from advanced study in the United States to civil war and
foreign invasion. They expected to play a pivotal role in shaping China's
future.

Unfortunately Mao Zedong had very little appreciation for foreign
experience, despite the fact that his chief lieutenant Zhou Enlai had been
on a work-study program in France. Intellectuals were never accorded the
respect or position given to pre-1949 scholars such as Hu Shi.

Some professors who embraced communism, for example Chen's
friend and mentor, Luo Longji, succumbed to infamy during the 1957 Anti-
Rightist campaign. Since Chen Renbing and Luo were politically aligned as
fellow members in the China Democratic League, Chen also was targeted
as the first "big rightists" vilified for their alleged treachery.

Some of the post-second world war period students who went to the
United States were supported by the Chinese government. Others used a
combination of private funds and fellowships from American schools.
After passing certain requirements, study abroad students were allowed to
buy foreign currency at a fixed official rate on the black market.

Roughly half of this group, mostly students of science and technology,
returned in a large group right after China's liberation between 1949 and
1952.

On August 24, 1954, the Communist Party was outlawed in the United States. After the outbreak of the Korean War, there was a regulation that no science, technology or engineering students could return directly home because it was feared that students would bring hydrogen bomb technology back to China.

The same anonymous friend of Chen Renbing who was accused of heading the Ku Klux Klan during the Cultural Revolution, told me that in this period of his study abroad the US army had even drafted him, a Chinese citizen, into military service!

Dr. Xie Xide, Chair of the Shanghai Committee of the Chinese People's Political Consultative Conference and Past President of Fudan University, studied at Smith College from 1947 to 1949 and at Massachusetts Institute of Technology from 1949 to 1952.

> When Dr. Xie talks about her life, typical of that of many intellectuals of her generation, it is clear that here is a woman of backbone. The daughter of a physicist who taught at Yenching University (now part of Peking University), she fled from Peking with her parents soon after the Japanese occupied Peking in July 1937. After wandering across half of China, her family reached Guiyang in remote Guizhou Province. Here she was ill and unable to move from her hospital bed for 4 years.
>
> Eventually she recovered, and attended Amoy University where her father had found a teaching post and which had been evacuated to the hill town of Changding in Fukien Province to escape the Japanese.
>
> In 1947 Dr. Xie sailed on a GI troopship from Shanghai to take up a scholarship at Smith College and later went on to Massachusetts Institute of Technology. Meanwhile, the Korean war had broken out, and Chinese "volunteers" had fought American troops when they crossed the 38th parallel and advanced to the Yalu River.
>
> Dr. Xie was determined to return to China, feeling that only there could she really be useful to her people. But in those days Washington was not allowing Chinese students to go home directly. Dr. Xie's fiancee, Dr. Cao, had just completed his studies in Britain, and she decided to join him there. The two were married and returned to their homeland via the Suez Canal and Singapore in October 1952. Ever since, Dr. Xie has been at Fudan University and her husband at the Shanghai branch of the Academy of Sciences.
>
> She was a part of the early post-World War II wave of Chinese students to the US—a group that included Nobel Prize-winners Yang Chenning[103] and Lee Tsungdao.[104]

Dr. Xie Xide said that in China's stage of development, when the whole country is still striving to lift itself out of perennial poverty and attitudes dating from the feudal past, "one needs more devotion to one's country than to one's own career." Through all the twists and turns of her own professional career, that is the motto she has lived by. "After all," she said, "do you not love your own mother, however poor she may be?"[105]

When Zhou En Lai attended the Geneva Convention in 1954, he did not shake hands with American delegate Alex Farnsworth. Nevertheless, an agreement was reached to exchange visiting Chinese scholars with American soldiers held as Korean war prisoners.

Automation engineer Dr. Tong Shibai graduated in 1951 from the University of Illinois. Dr. Tong experienced frustrations typical to scientists who attempted to leave the United States for China in the 1950s.[106] Investigated by the Federal Bureau of Investigation, Tong was asked if he was communist and what opinions he had about the war. Professor Tong said:

> It was difficult to get a job. They would not let us go back. After receiving my Ph.D., I got a ticket home but the dean of the graduate office said, 'I have news for you, you cannot go home.' The dean explained that there was one article for people at war, that the government could not allow them to go back. If we attempted to do so there was about a $5,000 fine and we would have to stay in jail for a while.

> To find a job was not so easy and with this situation it was very difficult. I also had some trouble living in New York with racism, not at the university, but, for instance, at barber shops sometimes they wouldn't serve me."

> Finally with the help of my advisors, I got job at the Brooklyn Polytechnic Institute, later called New York Polytechnic Institute. I worked there 3 years, until 1955 when Zhou Enlai worked out an arrangement with (John Foster)Dulles. China exchanged our students with American prisoners of war. At that time about 2,000 students were exchanged.

> The FBI called me again and tried to persuade us not to go back. The US did not want to admit that there were so many held in the US, closely watched, with our mail monitored. The immigration deportation office gave 3 weeks to leave and did not arrange transportation either by plane or boat.

> They tried to persuade me to become a US citizen. More than 50% of the students stayed. At that time, there were about 5,000 students from the mainland. The exchange took place from 1955-56. I had to ask a lawyer to take care of this and to make arrangements with my institute.

> The FBI man said, 'After all why go back? Is it because the Chinese Communist Party will give you a good job?'[107]

Governmental pressure was keenly felt by science students. Students of liberal arts or social sciences also felt apprehensive because relatives or friends warned them it was no use coming back. They heard about the Thought Reform Movement whereby an intellectual had to change ideologies before he or she was allowed to make any contributions.

Endnotes

1.   In a letter, Chen Renbing noted that the Taiping Kingdom's Christianity was, "In fact very immature and shallow. The Rebellion failed because of disunity, also the help of Christian countries like Britain and America contributed to the suppression of the Kingdom. General Gordon, no doubt a devout Christian, helped to speed the death of a God-worshipping movement."

2.   Immanuel C.Y. Hsu in The Rise of Modern China notes that the Taiping Rebellion 1850-1864 was the largest of three "debilitating internal convulsions" that nearly brought down the Qing dynasty. Root causes were continuous shrinking of landholdings, effects of the opium trade, political corruption, military degradation, and natural disasters. The rebellion started in the south, far away from the capital and more vulnerable to outside influences and Christianity.

3.   The two counties were named Huangpi and Xiaogang.

4.   Letter from Chen Renbing to J.F. Ford August 14, 1988.

5.   Chen Chunghai made a living as a maker of barrels, rice toons, washing basins, water carriers as well as rice steams held together with bamboo rings.

6.   Chen Renbing's father was referred to as Chen Chong Gui, Ch'eng Chong Kwei or Marcus Ch'eng. For the purpose of this study we will refer to him as Marcus Chen.

7.   Roberg, Ted, The Covenant Quarterly, Marcus Ch'eng and the Covenant China Mission February-May 1992, Vol. XLX, No. 1-2.

8.   In a letter to J.F. Ford September 17,1986 Chen Renbing wrote: I searched my memories of my fathers talks with me concerning his first wife, a nurse. These talks were held either in a hotel room in Shanghai in the summer of 1930 or in my apartment in Shanghai in 1958. They were so remote now. Since my father rushed down from the mountain resort of Guling, he must have had some sort of message, a letter or telegram, of his bride's critical state. My impression from these talks was that his bride of eight months was in her dying moment when my father got to her bedside at home and found that she was beyond saving. If my father arrived after her death, even a few hours or a day, I think I would not have written it the way I did. My father has said that after several years and not right then, when a bridegroom's huge sorrow had settled into more reason, he had suspected her illness to be consumption, not merely emotional pressure and pain from her mother-in-law.

9.   Jiang Jieshi took over the Nationalist government after Sun Zhongshan died in 1925. Jiang and Sun married sisters, Meiling and Qiling Sung, respectively and a wealthy financier Kong Xiangxi married the oldest Sung daughter, Eling. T.V. Sung, the girl's brother was a financier who, along with Kung, engineered the path of American aid and the domestic economy for Jiang's government. Generalissimo Jiang was in power during the Japanese invasion, civil war and World War II

10.   The year of Renbing's birth

11.   For reader's convenience, the English names of Chen's siblings are used.

12.   Roberg, Ted, The Covenant Quarterly, Marcus Ch'eng and the Covenant China Mission February-May 1992, Vol. XLX, No. 1-2.

13.   Marshall Feng Yu Xiang, Supervisor of China's Northwestern Border Defense, wanted to increase the number of troop chaplains from three or four to thirty or forty, to serve troops stationed from Beijing to Xian and Langzhou and north to Inner Mongolia.

To head the Christian Council for the Northwestern Army Feng finally recruited father as Chaplain General. Feng insisted that his chaplains be college graduates and ordained ministers. One day father said to me with a grin, " If I didn't happen to hold the Bachelor's degree from Wheaton, I wouldn't have met the minimum requirement here!"

Locally, in Zhang Jia Kou, troops were quartered in garrisons or houses commandeered for army use. Feng once said to my father and some friends, "Let me take you on a surprise inspection." It was two A.M. and they had just finished a long discussion. Feng randomly chose from the garrison list and the group arrived at the gate where the Marshall simply told the night guard to have the emergency duty order given by the commanding officer. They found everything was clean, well swept and polished. They repeated the random check at two other camps which mirrored perfect order.

All the deputy chaplains were unusually able men. One man, Theodore B. Tu, MS Columbia University, from was not a preacher himself, but was a trained singer and expert in church music. He even cut a RCA record of hymn solos. He fought against the Japanese as a Brigadier General in the Chinese Fifth Army under Marshall Fang Cheng Wu and died in 1937.

Deputy Chaplain Pu Huaren was an Episcopalian clergyman who later became a Communist. In both capacities he remained faithful and sincere. At his college graduation ceremony, my former teacher and principal, escorted his white-haired mother on stage and presented her with his diploma. Everyone applauded his gratitude and devotion. In 1948 Pu worked as a Liberation Army military court officer near Zhang Jia Kou. In 1950 he headed the People's University Foreign Language School in Beijing and later he headed the All China Relief Society. He was a much respected old cadre in the Communist Party.

Some houses were used as offices for Feng's Christian Council, others accommodated Nationalists delegates or warlord friends and even Communists, who usually had bona fide Nationalists credentials.

14.   Letter from Chen Renbing to J.F. Ford September 17, 1986

15.   For further reading consult the Concise History of Christianity published by China Encyclopedia Publishing Company, Shanghai Branch 1992 p.57-58 entry :'Chen Chong Gui 1883-1963', and, 'Honoring the Memory of Reverend Chen Chong Gui' written by the Three Self Patriotic Movement Committee written by 20 people including Chen Renbing and Chen Meida. 1991/2 Shanghai Publishing Company.

16.   Poteat, Gordon (1924) On Adapting Preaching to China in Home Letters From China p. 109

17.   Sun Zhongshan (Sun Yat-sen) 1866-1925 Sun became the first Chinese president of the new republic uniting a country of warlord fiefdoms after the dynasty fell in 1911. Chen Renbing based his beliefs on Sun Zhongshan's philosophy and a commitment to Western democratic ideals.

18.   Chen Renbing unpublished biography
19.   The school Principal Yui left China to study at Columbia University's Teacher's College and Reverend Pu was appointed his successor.
20.   Joel was in primary school, Renbing and Joses were in the second year of senior high 1925-26.
21.   Chen Renbing described the atmosphere and schedule of the Yu De School in his biography: "Joses and I were in our second year of high school, and Joel was in the high primary section. Feng managed to obtain use of one of former Emperor Chen Lung's summer palaces for our school compound.

It was simply wonderful to live within that miniature palace, where, enclosed behind a moon-like wall were houses, pagodas, temples and shaded monuments carved with calligraphy. Artificial mountains and decorative platforms made of bricks surrounded a moon-shaped lake, and its circumference measured exactly 3 "li" or 1 mile. Our routine for morning exercise was to run around the lake full circle. There was no short cut, unless you swam across midway because the athletic director ran with us and brought up the rear.

Feng's physical training appointees were among two or three of his most able captains and they were ordered by the Marshall himself not to be lenient and easy going. In winter, when ice formed, a few brave ones would slide across halfway, only to risk being discovered and ordered to begin all over again.

We little soldiers were issued rifles, and were responsible for the weapons and ammunition. In class, the rifles were erected beside the teacher's platform, three to a bunch. In the dormitory, the guns again stood in threes at the foot of our beds.

School principal was Yui Xing Xin, Anhui Province native and Nanjing Theological Seminary scholar. Yui spoke slowly and quietly when teaching us ethics and used as textbook, the Chinese translation of The Meaning of Service written by Reverend Fosdick of the New York City Riverside Church.

Principal Yui selected excellent teachers for our studies of Chinese classics, art, English and music. Our Chinese language teacher selected essays by Li Dazhao, Communist professor at Beijing University. I remember studying his essay, "Now" and one year later reading in Beijing newspapers about his execution by military warlord Chang Zuoling on April 28, 1927."

22.   Chen Renbing unpublished biography
23.   Chen Renbing admired Feng Yuxiang and his wife and detailed his personal knowledge of them. "Marshall Feng and his family used to live in one of the better built semi-Western style home near the Village entrance, but gave up his house for guests and moved to the inferior pressed mud cottages located in the back of the New Village. That was Feng's way, taking the less comfortable accommodations and deferring to his guests.

Even when Feng was deputy of the Nationalists Supreme Military Command he had a humble cottage built on a vacant lot next to the luxurious mansion built for Mayor Liu Qi Wen. Some daring municipal government controller found silk stocking purchases charged to the mayors account and made this spicy news item public. Mrs. Wen, attractive of face and figure, was dubbed "Mrs. Silk Stockings" in all the Shanghai and Guangzhou evening tabloids.

A few days after we arrived Feng invited our whole family for dinner. Children sat at one round table and adult at another for the my first western style dinner. We didn't fumble too much using forks and knives.

Feng strictly supervised his children's education and employed an old Chinese scholar to teach Chinese classics and calligraphy. Sometimes he locked his eldest boy in his room to insure concentrated study. The boy often sneaked out his window to play basketball, but upon hearing his father approach back in he would climb. Woe to him if he was caught!

Strict and industrious himself, Feng also studied with the bearded Chinese tutor. Both he and Mrs. Feng respectfully listened to lectures on the intricacies of the Book of Change and other Confucian classics. Carefully prepared cups of first grade green tea were placed in front of the master and his two attentive pupils. Marshall Feng delivered masterful talks to his men, his speech alive with native expressions of northern China and dotted not only with wit but sometimes filled with passion. Soon after Japan invaded Shanghai on January 28, 1937, I chaired a student meeting in the chapel of the University of Shanghai when Marshall Feng gave us a stirring speech.

Passion, not skepticism was the key word toward appreciating a man who was so often misunderstood by his contemporaries. In St. Matthew and St. Mark it was recorded that, "Jesus had compassion on the multitude" (Matt. 15:32 and Mark 8:2). I believe in human history we do find people who share other men's feelings and are at one with their suffering. In old China, among military lords great and small, one could not find a parallel to Feng Yu Xiang.

Mrs. Feng, nee Li Daquan, graduated from Methodist Women's College, and was General Secretary of the Beijing Y.W.C.A. when they married. Learned, eloquent and capable, she certainly was a wonderful match for the Christian General. One of her innovations was to set up a training class for officer's wives and grown daughters, many illiterate northern villagers. Miss Sun Hui Lang assisted Mrs. Feng in teaching Chinese, simple arithmetic as well as sewing, embroidering, housekeeping, home economics, child care and the Bible.

Two years later in 1927, Mrs. Feng established a girls junior high school in the impoverished western section of Beijing. She asked her YWCA successor Miss Minnie Wong MA Columbia Teacher's College, to become school principal. Years later Miss Wong married my uncle Matthew Chen through the matchmaking of the Fengs. As a distinguished Chinese women's movement leader, her career culminated in being elected as Vice President for the All China Political Consultative Council after liberation.

Dr. Liu Fang of the Beijing Methodist Church preceded my father as one of the network chaplains and our families were neighbors in line of new one story houses in Feng's 'New Village'. Regular Sunday worship service was held in a 800 seat auditorium in the village center and I appointed myself organist."

24.	Chen Renbing unpublished biography
25.	"Evangelism" periodical founded by Marcus. A monthly in connection with Stewart Fund. Marcus became editor of this monthly for many years well into the forties, as a family enterprise. Renbing and Joses were co-editors beside Marcus as editor-in-chief subscription of more than 20,000.
26.	The Chens moved to the counties of Wanxian and Kaixian.
27.	Chen Renbing unpublished biography
28.	Chen Renbing was impressionable and his version of the World's Fair was 'This Hollywood theater depicted how a movie was filmed and produced. Country folks from Montana or states in the Deep South could see how glamorous actresses and actors worked, how camera operators, directors, script writers actually make

a pictures. A beautiful girl in tatters was saved from the mouth of a tiger, barely in time, by a Tarzan in leopard skin. The director would emerge from the shadowy sideline to shout "Cut", then, order a retake. They performed this show perhaps six times a day. The vogue of the Nation, "The Fan Dance of Sally Rand" drew audiences day and night. Lights dimmed to almost complete darkness. Suddenly, a soft spotlight revealed shapely Miss Rand with two huge feather fans her only covering as she pulsated to sensuous rhythms. Only split second "fanning" over her nude body kept police from taking hold of her.

Near Miss Rand's show and the "Hollywood" doings, an overseas Catonese sold lichee nuts and sundry Chinese souvenirs to tourists. For a few dollars a week, Pearl hired on as his assistant, and she convinced the pedlar to let me work salary-free, except for a World's Fair employee pass. I got to keep Pearl's company and I did all I could to boost the old man's meager business. It goes without saying that I often looked in on the "Fan Dance" free of charge! The booth sold bamboo chopsticks that people took home to show folks back in Dakota or Virginia what Chinese used instead of a knife and fork. The chopsticks did not sell well, so, I posted a sign saying, "Your name translated into Chinese and written on your chopsticks free of charge." Some people bought 10 pairs at a time, and, I would oblige with translations of Marcelo, Claudia, Mark, Kathleen, Rose, Edward, Mary, Francis and Barbara, et cetera, written in Chinese ink. We sold them by the dozen. Of course, I wrote down the English name too, otherwise they wouldn't know which name fit what Chinese characters. I can still hear the throbbing music, the kettle drums rolling for a daredevil who, several times a day, walked over a tight wire strung high over the Fair lagoon, his blindfolded eyes heightening the audience's suspense. No accident ever befell that performer, but I always recall how tense I felt watching him. I said to myself, "I'm glad I don't have to earn my daily bread (or bowl of rice) that way!"

29.   Chen Renbing unpublished biography
30.   Chen Renbing unpublished biography
31.   Chen wrote: "I am indebted to Michigan not only because it has given me advanced education in sociology, but also it opened my eyes and ears to the world of western music. As a tenor, I enrolled in Assistant Professor Hamilton's voice class. I rented a piano at our Thayer Street apartment, thus making our life extraordinarily frugal but rich. I sang not only masterpieces by Shubert and Schumann, but also works by Chinese composers Chao Yuan Jen, Hwang Tze and others. Pearl and I joined the 350 voice Michigan Choral Union, composed of students, faculty and local residents under the baton of the Music School Director.

We performed annual concerts of great choral works like "The Seasons", "The Magic Mountain" or "The Creation" and had Dr. Stock of the Chicago Symphony Orchestra or Stowkowski of the Philadelphia Symphony as guest conductors.

The three Christmases we were in Ann Arbor, Dr. Stock conducted Handel's Messiah accompanied by our own University Symphony of 150 artists . . . As Choral Union member we were entitled free admission to grand concerts given by some of the world's greatest musicians. It was no less than a blessing to hear Heifetz, Krisler, Iturbe, Rachmaninoff, Rubenstein, Rose Ponselle, Lily Pons and Martinelli in person. The Michigan Music Hall seated 5,000 and Pearl and I indeed were among the lucky, hearing almost all the first symphonies in the United States as well.

32.   Sometime in 1934, an American motion picture company was contemplating casting a Chinese to star as male lead in Pearl Buck's The Good Earth. When the first of several scouting deputations came to canvas Michigan students likely for screening, I tried out. In any case, the movie people looked me over and went away. I never did know just how much chance I stood, they certainly canvassed a wide range of Chinese students and finally gave up the idea of using a Chinese for the role

33.   Chen Renbing unpublished biography

34.   I am greatly indebted to Dr. Foster and his wife for their 1992 interviews while on holiday in Sarasota, Florida. In a letter of October 26, 1992, Foster wrote 'I received a letter in the late 1950s from Mrs. Chen asking for my help in her getting a job in the Mankato State College Biology Department.' He was unable to help her and lost touch with her. The Fosters have lived in Mankato, MN since 1952.

35.   Chen Renbing unpublished biography

36.   Ann paid Chen Renbing a visit September 8,9,10, 1986 with husband and youngest daughter after 39 years of separation.

37.   From December 4, 1941 to December 4, 1943, Marcus Chen lived in Malaya, a period covered in his book, *Escape from Singapore*. Afterwards he became President of the Zhongqing Theological Seminary with the support of Bishop Frank Houghton of the China Inland Mission. In 1943 Marcus went back to Zhongqing in southwestern China and from 1944-1945 lived in Yibing, Sichuan Province. He returned to Zhongqing in 1945 and from 1948 to December 1949 he visited the United States and Europe with Mrs. Chen.

38.   First, Nationalists spies killed a student named Yu Zi San at Zhejiang University in Hangzhou on October 29,1947. A hundred thousand people demonstrated for freedom and against intimidation in Hangzhou, Beijing, Tianjin, Shanghai, Nanjing, Kunming, and school strikes were commonplace. The second protest wave, Anti-Hunger and Anti-Suppression" demonstrations, broke out in major cities, including Chengdu, in April 1948.

39.   On the evening of May 22, 1948, a group of 15,000 teachers and students met on the football grounds of Jiaotung University, protesting American aid to Japanese militarist forces and Jiang Jieshi's anti-democratic government. Chen Renbing was invited to be the sole speaker at the 5- hour long rally featuring parades and demonstrators singing the Communist pep song, "You Are the Light Tower." A torch parade wound around the grounds while a few thousand Nationalists agents surrounded the University, preventing the huge crowd from spilling out into the streets

40.   Chen Renbing biography chapter 17

41.   Chen Renbing unpublished biography

42.   Chi Wen Shun, Readings in Chinese Communist Documents, University of California Press 1968 pp. 188-189

43.   November 20, 1945 New York Times

44.   October 3, 1946 New York Times

45.   10/24/47, 10/26/47, New York Times

46.   October 28, 1947 New York Times

47.   January 6, 1947 New York Times

48.   Including Professor Wu Han

49.   Also in attendance at the meeting were Professors Chang Zhirang, Pan Chenya, Mr. T.L. Shen

50.   Chen Renbing unpublished biography

51.   Chen Renbing unpublished biography

52.   Chen Renbing unpublished biography

53.   Roberg, Ted, The Covenant Quarterly, Marcus Ch'eng and the Covenant China Mission February-May 1992, Vol. XLX, No. 1-2.

54.   This organization was chaired by Mr. Y.T. Wu, well known for Christian activities in the Chinese YMCA.

55.   Concise History of Christianity published by China Encyclopedia Publishing Company, Shanghai Branch 1992, pp. 57-58

56.   Chen Renbing unpublished biography

57.   Marcus visited Gansu, Shanxi, Hubei and Hunan provinces.

58.   The verbatim speech is found in Donald E. MacInnis Religious Policy and Practice in Communist China, 1972 NY, p. 201. The Macmillian Co.

59.   Chen Renbing unpublished biography

60.   Chen Renbing unpublished biography.

61.   I am indebted to Ted Roberg for this information. See Roberg, T. Marcus Ch'eng and the Covenant China Mission The Covenant Quarterly Vol. XLX, Nos.1-2 February-May 1992 p.8, 12, 13.

62.   I am indebted to Ted Roberg for this information. See Roberg, T. Marcus Ch'eng and the Covenant China Mission The Covenant Quarterly Vol. XLX, Nos.1-2 February-May 1992 p.8, 12, 13.

63.   The Covenant Quarterly February-May 1992 Vol. XLX, Nos. 1-2. p.3

64.   Chen Renbing unpublished biography

65.   Tianjin General Hospital was where their Uncle Matthew was superintendent.

66.   Chen Renbing unpublished biography

67.   Letter from Chen Renbing to J.F. Ford 9/17/88

68.   Chen Renbing unpublished biography

69.   Letter from Chen Renbing to J.F. Ford 9/17/88

70.   Interview with Chen Meida Thursday June 18, 1992 at her home near Lu Xun Gong Yuan

71.   In a letter from Chen Renbing to J.F. Ford on September 17, 1986

72.   Interview with Chen Meida

73.   Mr. K.C. Wu, the former mayor of Zhongqing and Shanghai

74.   Chen Renbing unpublished biography

75.   Chen Renbing unpublished biography

76.   Chen Renbing unpublished biography

77.   Chen notes that "The Garrison Commander for the Nationalist army announced that he would hold Fuzhou for 3 years against the Communists, and Pearl believed him. However, Fuzhou did not last 3 years, but only 5 months."

78.   Chen Renbing unpublished biography

79.   Chen Renbing unpublished biography

80.   Chen found out later that Pearl had been on the faculty at Albion College.

81.   Interview with Chen Meida

82.   Dr. Chen Renbing's mother's youngest sister. She was married to Lo Yi Nong who is profiled in the Pocket Dictionary of History published by Wuhan Normal College History Department in January, 1980. The articles entitled, "In

Memory of Comrade Lo: Crimson Blood Over Longhua" and "Red Flowers Bloom Over China", were written by Madame Li in the People's Daily of May 13, 1982.

83.   Li Wenyi letter to J.F. Ford July 6, 1992
84.   Chen Renbing unpublished biography
85.   Chen Renbing unpublished biography
86.   Letter to J.F. Ford 92/7/6
87.   June 7, 1992 letter from Li Wenyi to J. F. Ford
88.   Letter to J. F. Ford 1982
89.   Chen Renbing unpublished biography
90.   Chen Renbing unpublished biography
91.   Chen Renbing unpublished biography
92.   Chen Renbing unpublished biography
93.   Chen Renbing unpublished biography
94.   Chen Renbing unpublished biography
95.   On Fudan University campus, Number Four dormitory housed the author and other foreign students in 1980-82. The dormitory Dr. Chen is referring to was located directly across from our building. The front portion of the building housed a laundry service and other rooms were used as Chinese student dormitories.
96.   Chen Renbing unpublished biography
97.   Chen Renbing unpublished biography
98.   Lin Biao, veteran of the Long March and former defense minister, died in a plane crash in 1971 after he had allegedly tried to kill Mao in an assassination attempt
99.   Chen Renbing unpublished biography
100.   Letter to J.F. Ford 1992
101.   Chen Renbing unpublished biography
102.   Letter from Chen Renbing to J. F. Ford
103.   Dr. Yang Chenning, a noted physicist, is on the faculty of the State University of Stony Brook and was instrumental in developing the exchange program between SUNY Stony Brook and Fudan University of which the author was the first Stony Brook participant.
104.   Christian Science Monitor article, Monday March 26, 1984 Xie Xide-the gentle president of China's Fudan University.
105.   Christian Science Monitor article, Monday March 26, 1984 Xie Xide-the gentle president of China's Fudan University.
106.   1948-1951 Ph.D. University of Illinois
107.   Interview with Tong Shibai 1982/5/10 at Qinghua University

1. *1936 The Chen Family in Changsha. Back row left to right:*
Mary, Joses, Joel, John (Renbing) and Martha.
Front row: Miriam, Mother, Father, Joshua.

2. *1937 Spring. Chen family portrait taken in front of their Changsha home.*
Standing left to right back row: Joses, Pearl, John (Renbing) holding Ann, Joel.
Second row standing: Mary, Miriam, Joshua and Martha.
Sitting: Father and Mother.

3. *1933 Chen Renbing standing in front of the School of Philosophy at the University of Southern California after being conferred a MA in Sociology.*

4. *1933 Chen Renbing in Chicago.*

5. *1933 Chen Renbing in Los Angeles.*

6. *1935 Newlyweds Chen Renbing and Pearl Liu Chen in Ann Arbor, Michigan*

7. *1935 Chen Renbing and Pearl at their home
210 Thayer Street, Ann Arbor, Michigan.*

8. *1938 Chen Renbing in Hong Kong with the Wuhan Songsters. On the back of the photograph is stamped: "Way Hay College Student's War Relief Association."*

9. 1936 "Welcome" decoration in front of the family gate in Wuchang upon
the return of Chen Renbing as Ph.D. in conformity with the old Chinese custom
of celebrating the elevation of sons or grandsons to National Examination honors.
For such occasions, monuments were erected at ancestral shrines or in the clan village.

Chapter III: China Under Mao Zedong

Overseas Chinese students greeted allied victory in 1945 with exhilaration.[1] Young intellectuals who decided to study in the United States, rather than in Europe or Japan, felt comfortable with progressive social philosophers like John Dewey and liberal Western ideology. One intellectual expressed high hopes for initial efforts of reforming China after WW II:

> Bit by bit, we felt the Communist Party might be the right party to lead China. Everyone had something to eat. Bandits and bad forces were swept away. There were no prostitutes then. We also saw that the foreign forces in the British Concession in Shanghai controlled all customs, post offices, electricity and gas companies. It seems that they were the master of our destiny. The Communist Party came and got rid of that master. That was amazing because the foreign forces then were strong. I really expressed my admiration for the Party.

> Regarding their way of thinking, the Communists were too conservative. They thought that intellectuals were extremely revolutionary. That really made me crazy, but I could not help it. As time went by, it seemed there was only one road for us to take. We finally consecrated our lives to the Communist Party. We had no objections to whatever the Party commanded. Wherever they directed us to go, we obeyed. I thought it was nice.

> Gradually, I realized that all the cadres, government officials were worthy of admiration. They always put other interests before their own. They were really humble servants of the people. A government composed of such people was much better that of the Nationalists. Sometimes the Communists Party went to extremes. For example, they took all missionaries for spies. We could not agree with them on that. But, that was the case.

> We found that Mao Zedong Thought could tackle many problems aris-
> ing from erroneous thinking. For example, before we didn't know why
> we studied music. The only knowledge we had about music then was
> "art for art's sake" or "art for living". On campus, everyone had their
> own view. After liberation, Mao Zedong Thought advocated serving
> the people. This advocacy really worked. I lived to serve the people and
> I learned to serve the people. This served as the aim of my life. Mao
> Zedong Thought also had a great influence upon our thinking. We
> used to get confused with the material dialectics. We had some ideas
> about how to cope with problems dialectically and historically. The
> knowledge of Mao Zedong Thought made our original ideas move.[2]

Obviously, Chen Renbing was impressed with Mao, because Mao spoke of
ideologies which appealed to Chen's sense of "democratic idealism". At an
Imperial Palace[3] reception for newly elected Central Executive Committee
members, Chen Renbing recalled "Mao took time to evaluate dogmatism
and empiricism, saying both were 'no good'. Mao said, 'one didn't need to
slaughter 500 pigs before one was able to kill a pig,' yet on the other hand,
'theories without practice were always dangerous."[4] Mao and Dewey dif-
fered but United States-trained intellectuals could find common ground in
Mao's dialectical materialism and Dewey's criticism of dogma that "there
is a kind of idle theory which is antithetical to practice." Intellectuals
appreciated the idea that "genuinely scientific theory falls within practice
as the agency of its expansion and its direction to new possibilities."[5]

Mao's revolutionary model held that classes could be suspended so
teachers and students alike could join political-ideological campaigns or
participate at the production front. Mao's paradigm attracted those who
accepted the Deweyan emphasis on the importance of experience when
"the whole society educates" and learning takes place at the farm, in the
factory or on the street.[6]

Intellectuals may have been willing to consider that in republican
China, Dr. Hu Shi, Columbia University graduate and spokesperson for
John Dewey, was wrong to tell students[7] to dissociate themselves with
Anti-Japanese protests and resume classes towards acquiring conservative
and mature outlooks. Later, as a western oriented scholar Hu believed that
the Communist party should establish a system to protect and help the
writer, but not to command him. Mao wanted to counter intellectuals
influenced by Deweyan ideas of pragmatism and practical applications of
theory. When Mao targeted Hu Shi it revealed that Mao held intellectuals
suspect for undermining the changes he deemed necessary to "cleanse"
China of Western influence. Attacks escalated in 1956 when Mao encouraged intellectuals to express "free thought" and tried to get them to lead
society to a common ideology. However, their right to exercise opinions
brought questions and criticisms to communist ideology.

As world and domestic issues prevailed, reform movements to "improve conditions" within China gave way to ideological issues. Intellectuals who probably considered themselves apolitical "were afraid of the Communists at first because we had the facts in favor of the Nationalists, which were supposed to be wrong. But we had the impression that the Communists were atheistic, against religion."[8] Fears turned to reality when Mao decided the way to curb thought[9] through anti-intellectual movements during Chen Renbing's lifetime. Some prominent campaigns included: The Suppress Counterrevolutionary Movement (1949), Resist America-Aid Korea campaign (1950-52) Anti-Hu Feng[10] Movement (1953), Thought Reform Movement (1953- 1958) Anti-Rightist Movement (1957) and, the Cultural Revolution (1966- 1976).

In Mao's scheme[11] being "red" was more desirable than being "expert." Until 1958 the party line was "the proletariat must have its own intelligentsia". Mao turned away from the academic program of Soviet advisors and promoted a blend of revolutionary and academic models where politics and ideological commitment carried more weight than professional qualifications in hiring and promotion of teachers.[12]

Chen Renbing spent time and energy garnering financial and political support in Nanjing as a China Democratic League liaison man in anticipation of the Communist victory. Chen revealed positive feelings he and other intellectuals had during the first few days of Mao's China.

> The first Liberation soldiers entered Nanjing and by April 21, Nanjing was an empty city. Nationalists troops withdrew clean before. The take-over went on smoothly causing one to suspect careful planning behind all these activities. Two weeks later, I was invited to a dinner hosted by Marshall Liu Bocheng,[13] field army head. A pair of round tables were set for dinner. Other invited guests[14] had been on good terms with liberal professors and patriotic students.

> Another gentleman, the President of Nanjing University, was conspicuously absent from the guest list because he actively participated in the bogus National Congress. Famous scholar, Dr. Hu Shi[15] and Catholic Bishop Yu Pin earned their notoriety through their role in presenting the illegitimate "Constitution" to President Jiang Jieshi at the climax of the disputed Congress.[16] Some lines of demarcation could not be overlooked.

> The vacant seat at my right was filled by Marshall Liu who said, "No one is host for today's dinner. Everybody present is the host." He talked briefly about the meaning of liberation and educational conditions before liberation. To illustrate his point that, in the past, graduating from college meant becoming unemployed, he recited a Chinese couplet "A dead end after all : All chance of a living has ceased." The beauty of the couplet is that the first character of each six character

sentence, namely the words "bi" and "ye", form the Chinese verb "graduate", while the content of the couplet describes hopelessness. Marshall Liu continued, speaking of future abundance and prosperity.

Several professors expressed welcome to the People's Army and the joy of being reunited with "our own troops." One guest[17] admired the Communist's strict discipline, saying he was anxious that their purity never be diluted.

It was clear that the hearts of Chinese liberal intellectuals had been won over by the Communists. Men like Marshall Liu could really make you feel at home in their company. Nationalist generals had scarcely achieved one hundredth of this.[18]

Chen Renbing recounted one of the most unforgettable experiences of his life, a reception Mao Zedong gave at the Imperial Palace.

Mao commented[19] on the national public debt notes recently floated by the government. Explaining that we had to take care of the tens of thousands of officials left over from Jiang Jieshi's government, he said, "All of them have got digestive systems. We cannot expect Truman or Marshall to feed them."

Speaking of unity and cooperation between comrades, Mao said that Communists were well experienced in such matters. A wise formula was, with unity as a starting point, pass through discussion (fighting or arguing) and go back to unity, that's the whole process, the secret of unity.

He dwelt on the importance of tactics in criticizing a friend. 'Before you list a friend's shortcomings one, two and three, you mention his good points one, two and three. He will be glad to hear the rest.'

When we finally said goodbye to him, he stood at the door at looked at us until we were quite some distance away. That was a memorable night for many of us who met the Chairman for the first time, although all of us had read a lot of his writings. For a long time that night I couldn't sleep for being excited and happy. Possibly I was not the only one who felt excited.

As I write this, I also recall that out of the 90 some persons present that night, about one third were capped rightists in the 1957 movement prompted by the Chairman.[20]

Mao realized twin goals, revolution and development, in a unique combination of a school-centered academic model which was knowledge oriented and produced scholars, as well as a society-centered revolutionary model which was action-centered and produced active revolutionaries.

Questions the communists decided were, "Should intellectuals be judged according to their political-ideological qualifications before they become acceptable for service in a proletarian society", and, "Is Confucius to be honored or condemned?"[21]

PERSONALIZED TARGETS AND THE CHINESE INTELLECTUAL TRADITION

Scholars have a dual responsibility not only to carry out duties but also an obligation to advise and remonstrate leaders. The label of "intellectual" in China represents a person who places high value on or pursues things of interest to the intellect or the more complex forms and fields of knowledge, such as aesthetic or philosophical matters, especially on an abstract and general level and believes that scholarly knowledge should eventuate in action and action should influence knowledge.[22] Chen Renbing's generation "turned inward on its own cultural tradition and outward toward the modern West"[23] in search of China's position in the modern world when revolutionary changes touched aspects of the nation's political, economic and social structures.[24] Returned overseas students came to be targeted because they reflected influences tempered by their embrace of western ideologies.

The Chinese intellectual tradition[25] springs from the collective experience of the people. "The Chinese people from the beginning always were oppressed. From the time of the Taiping Heavenly Kingdom to the establishment of the People's Republic of China, Chinese people were controlled by emperors, and felt the dynasty's oppression. Therefore from the time we are children, we just have one request that our country will have the heart to rise up and be strong.[26] We were, of one heart one mind, patriotic."[27]

Leaders of the democratic parties bore important duties in the new government. In August, Chen returned to liberated Shanghai to assume temporary duty as Democratic League chairman. In time, he was also elected a member of the Shanghai Political Consultative Council. Chen Renbing described one of the first political campaigns after 1949:

> The 'Three Opposition Movement' was intended to oppose corruption and waste. Later, there was also a movement opposing irregularities and illegal activities in business and industrial circles, such as tax evasion, producing sub-standard goods and other actions detrimental to the people's economic interests, collectively called the Five Opposition Movement. All Shanghai business and industrial establishments were surveyed and classified into one of five categories 1) law abiding 2) essentially law abiding 3) half law abiding 4) slight infringement of the law and 5) serious infringement of the law.

> A certificate was issued to each and every shop and factory. For those
> who violated financial or tax laws, a special court called The Shanghai
> People's Court for Handling of Five Opposition Cases was estab-
> lished.[28] I was appointed 1 of the 17 judges. I remember being allotted
> a case in which a manufacturer was accused of making poor quality
> machine equipment for a water reservoir contract in Anwei Province.[29]

Chen remained in Nanjing until August. "I was appointed vice chairman of
the local Democratic League branch. Many new members were added to
our roll and we worked at new proposals for changes in educational institutions. There was no end of work to do in transforming an underground
party into a partner with the party in power. After liberation, the League
found itself a member of united cause built around it's big Communist
brother."[30]

Now, 14 months after being fired from St. John's University, Chen was
invited to return as Professor of Political Science and Dean of the Liberal
Arts College, a post formerly held by William Pott, son of the old institution's founder. During the next 3 years at St. John's Chen taught political
science courses, offered lectures on the History of Social Development and
a course on New Democracy. Aside from teaching, much of his time was
spent doing China Democratic League work.[31]

Chen Renbing traveled yearly to Beijing meetings from 1949 to 1957.
In 1949, at the China Democratic League convention, Chen had a rare
opportunity of listening to Premier Zhou Enlai speak on the League's history and growth.

> He divided our history into four periods and commented on the
> progress and stumbling of each. We sat in two circles of sofas while
> Zhou stood in the middle. Except for a 15-minute break, Zhou spoke
> for 4 hours straight, without notes. During the rest, I took out my
> name card and scribed some words and had the card forwarded to him.
> He turned around in his seat and asked who sent the "little missile."
> Someone pointed at me and Zhou gave me a nod. A week later, at some
> consultation where Zhou and five or six other people were present, he
> mentioned my name and quoted the contents of my little message.[32]

Chen checked cases of counter-revolutionary criminals in the Shanghai's
People's Court responsible to the Shanghai People's Political Consultative
Council.[33] In 1951, a mass rally attended by 12,000 people was held in the
former Kenedrome of Shanghai and Chen spoke on behalf of the
Committee of Examinations of Counter-revolutionary Cases.

> In my address, I did not limit myself to case statistics and Committee
> decisions suggesting retrials. I also spoke to the importance of sup-
> pressing counter-revolutionaries which fell into two classes, spies the
> Nationalists planted when they escaped to Taiwan and local bandits
> who victimized farmers and townspeople, including ruffians and gang
> leaders in Shanghai who, with Nationalists protection before liberation,

committed crimes against the people. Everyone knew that Jiang Jieshi ordered spies, closely connected to underworld gangsters, to kill huge numbers of political prisoners.

I said that the Shanghai people demanded these criminals be brought to justice. The government motto concerning the Movement to Suppress Counter-revolutionaries was: 'Of those who deserve imprisonment, Not one should be released. Of those who deserve execution, Not one should be spared.'

People's sentiment dictated that we should war against these elements 'With banners unfurled and drums rumbling'. Therefore, my closing remarks were, 'Let us unfurl the Banner of Five Stars and Roll Onward the People's Drums.'[34]

Chen Ren Bing modeled himself after his friend Dr. Luo Longji, Chinese liberal intellectual, essayist, editorialist, publicist and politician during four decades.[35] Both men received their "formative schooling in the days when liberal values became widely disseminated on the campuses of schools and universities and championed a liberal alternative in China." Luo, "the last gasp of his generation of Chinese intellectuals" was an influence during a time of "crushing social, economic and political demands of a country devastated by sectarian strife, war, poverty, ignorance and spiritual decay". Intellectuals followed the ongoing debate between Hu Shi and Li Tazhao (Li Dazhao) the advocate of 'fundamental solutions' on a scale of the Bolshevik Revolution.[36]

Communist party enmity toward Dewey and Hu Shi began when Russia was the only major power to acknowledge China's legitimacy at the end of WW I. Before the Versailles Treaty was signed, liberal Chinese intellectuals hoped that the West would treat China fairly but support for Wilson and the League of Nations evaporated when reports[37] from France broke that China was still going to be carved up and handed to Germany and Japan. Since Dewey's strong support of President Wilson was well-known and unpopular among some intellectuals, Russia's Soviet policy initiative attracted attention and followers after Dewey was criticized.[38]

One popular writer[39] was criticized because he "consistently stood for the 'reactionary educational theories of John Dewey and American imperialism. Educators joined in criticizing his educational ideas and in demanding the elimination of 'Dewey's insidious influence' on educational thinking in China." Three volumes of an anti-Hu Shi collection were republished[40] charging that:

What Hu Shi expounded was the reactionary bourgeois idealism of imperialism, especially the reactionary pragmatism of John Dewey and William James. Therefore, to remove the prevailing malignancy Hu Shi's ideology caused from our academic world is of major significance to the task of opposing idealist ideology that serves modern imperialism.[41]

Skeptical intellectuals still wanted to remain in China after 1949, and accepted transfers to other institutions during Soviet-style educational reorganization. It was said that Mao[42] began changing the meaning of intellectual tradition, and "wanted to change one's heart, mind, the individual's 'ism.'" This was very unfair.[43] Chinese intellectuals, who returned home from studying in the United States, agree that the Chinese Communist Party hardly ever believed in them.

RESIST AMERICA-AID KOREA CAMPAIGN

In 1951, Chen recalled, the United Nations army was about to cross the Yalu River and the situation was critical. On October 25, all democratic parties of China, headed by the Communist Party, signed a united declaration announcing that Volunteers to North Korea would be dispatched in support of General Kim Il Sun.

> The first 'Comfort Team',[44] comprised of all democratic parties, people's organizations and Volunteer family representatives, went to North Korea. From October 16 to November 2, 1952, I was appointed a delegate in a similarly composed group and we, as did the group before us, brought along teams of musicians, dramatists, acrobats, magicians and other artists to entertain the Volunteers. We numbered a little over 1,000 people, and were led by famous actors.[45] It was the most unforgettable half month in my life.

> On the Korean fields I met quite a number of my former St. John's University students. Proficient in English, most of them worked as interpreters in prisoner of war camps. A few pupils told me of the privations and hardships encountered when they crossed the Yalu River. They graduated from another experience of far more immense dimensions.

> One of our duties was to pay respect to local Koreans and the People's Army of Chosen. We also visited many local women's societies. Although southern aggression had impoverished them, the poorly dressed Korean children were lovely. One group of little girls performed for us wearing silk dresses, silk made from U.S. parachutes!

> The Chinese Volunteers were really happy to see folks from back home. We talked to them of recent production, education and cultural progress in China, while they related valiant stories and fruits of victory. We met ever so many war heroes and model soldiers, many who asked us to sign their notebooks.

> I saw on one of the model soldier's notebooks a newspaper clipping
> showing Chairman Mao on the Tian An Men platform, holding hands
> with a boy and girl wearing red scarves. This fellow pasted pictures of
> his son and daughter alongside, making four children under Mao's
> wing.

The owner of that notebook was thinking of the children of China, including his precious ones, all cherished by the Great Chairman. I can never forget the night we bid farewell to a host Korean family, their friendly faced
silhouetted in the door frame, candles in hand, gently waving their hands
goodbye. I can still see the happy, honest faces of Volunteers, brave, ingen-
ious and ever loyal to China.

THE THOUGHT REFORM MOVEMENT AND EDUCATIONAL REORGANIZATION

Just as intellectuals were coming to grips with Mao's leadership, the
Thought Reform Movement was beginning mass mobilization movements.

> The first movement was land reform. Gradually we came to realize that
> the Communist party was not so terrible as expected. The second was
> ideological remolding. I feel that the Communists were very demand-
> ing. We could hardly bear it. You had to tell your history either good
> or bad in minute details. This really hurts one's feelings. Unfortunately
> there is no way to escape.

> One had to report everything including your history. They would not
> believe you the first two times. One could have a narrow escape after
> having his ideology remolded after four times. The Communist Party
> hardly ever believed in us. They tried to investigate our history and crit-
> icize us in the midst of our ideological remolding. Some criticism we
> could bear and some we could not.[46]

Resentment grew about indoctrination meetings led by poorly educated
party cadres with concomitant protracted discussions about ideology.
Intellectuals were exhorted to change habitual outlooks and thoughts to a
point where emotions were more important than knowledge acquisition or
the development of the intellect. Mao's objective was to produce a proletarian intelligentsia, not an intellectual elite. Knowledge was useful to the
extent that it was pertinent to production and politics. Dependence on foreign models and foreign materials was scorned and intellectuals were
downgraded not only by stripping them of the authority and status but by
requiring them to learn from workers, peasants and soldiers in the classroom as well as on the production site.[47]

Chen Renbing's friend and colleague[48] said, "We intellectuals are of
one heart and one mind, we love our country. Professor Chen loved his

country so much, to the point of "losing his mind" over her. It doesn't matter if the motherland treats us fairly or not. We just hope that China can do well, it's enough. We need nothing at all. This is quite remarkable." "There was no question of remaining out of politics as did some of his fellow liberal intellectuals.[49] He took the idea of political activism very seriously."[50]

Journalist Lu Yi, who got to know Chen Renbing during their incarceration at the Socialist Reeducation College in Shanghai during the Anti-Rightist Movement,[51] said that

> Chen Renbing had an open mind. Towards people he was honest and open. Towards his classmates he was the same. His thinking was liberated. In America, he developed ideas of people's freedom and democracy. But, when he came back to China, people were very feudalistic, close minded, inward looking. All of them were farmers, very conservative." Mr. Lu continued that, "China's history has always been opposing the emperor, fighting against feudal history. From the time of Sun Zhongshan, progress has been very slow, democracy is so limited. Chinese history is like a winding river.[52]

Chen Renbing merited socialism for creating optimism, "Since China had just stepped into liberation, the object in view seemed limited; cleaning from the Chinese intellectual's mind the influence of feudal, semi-feudal and imperialist ideologies, and introducing people's democratic doctrines. Patriotism was emphasized, honesty and integrity were valued virtues."[53] Party leaders, bolstered by the view that the correctness of Marxist-Leninist Thought had been verified in daily life, encouraged intellectuals to accept Marxism-Leninism as the spirit of Chinese social life and direction of the country. The Communist Party felt a responsibility to help intellectuals embrace self-education and socialist remolding willingly, whether they assented or not.

Chen wrote an article for the *China Review* on the Thought Reform Movement which took place from the winter of 1951 to the autumn of 1952 and dubbed it:

> another important phase of intellectual's experience after China's liberation which followed in sequence to the problems of administrative personnel highlighted in the Three Opposition Movement. The general idea of the Thought Reform Movement was the establishment in post-Liberation China of a Study Movement, somewhat modeled after the Study Movement of the Yenan days, when weapons of criticism and self-criticism were used to build up a worker's world outlook. To my mind, the Thought Reform Movement was aimed at establishing a systematic world outlook of socialism for Chinese intellectuals.[54]

> "Thought reform means reforming individual thinking. Do you think it would be difficult to change my thinking? If I want to reform you it

is also not easy. This situation is pitiful because intellectuals have self respect. To reform this kind of thinking hurts intellectual's self-respect. Thinking requires being turned inside out, having a look at the facts. Socialism really had the ability to elevate people's lifestyle, to really be able to build a better foundation for our country. So, thought reform, all over the country, what was called "brainwashing", couldn't do it. It just doesn't work."[55]

During the course of the Thought Reform Movement, if an intellectual expressed the idea to "make good friends everywhere and read good books," the Party would suggest that "good books" are those of Marxism-Leninism and dialectics. "Good friends" are the masses of workers peasants and laboring intellectuals. The Thought Reform Movement meant to tap intellectual's zeal for socialist politics and change a "one room and two books" mentality of contemplative research to a new outlook based on achieving an elevated political consciousness through ideological remolding.

Chen Renbing wrote of another intellectual who was initially inspired by the Thought Reform Movement:

Sometime in the spring of 1952, a gentleman was invited to speak before the assembly of St. John's University students and teachers. Professor L., from another Shanghai university, well known scholar and author of *The Development of Chinese Literature*, came to bear witness to the benefits he gained from the current movement to uplift moral integrity and absolute honesty. He said that he had not been straight in relating his personal history.

Professor L. used to tell people that he was trained in Paris, but, it came to light that he had never been to France. He felt ashamed and jumped into the Huang Pu River while crossing on a ferry boat, and was saved from drowning by fellow passengers. He wanted to share his experience of having gone astray and coming to know the right path of life, confessing that vanity led to his dishonesty. He had a new outlook on life, an outlook compatible with new, socialist China.

That was many years ago. The Thought Reform Movement lasted less than 2 years. Professor L. was among my friends. Five years later in the 1957 Anti-Rightist Campaign, he barely got by. His standing during the Cultural Revolution was dubious. All that can be said about him was he died a natural death in the late 1970's.[56]

Thought Reform Movement cadres sought to uncover fundamental reasons prohibiting intellectual from embracing politics. First to blame, was a general sense that intellectuals felt it unnecessary to worry about national affairs because government leadership could be followed with peace of mind. Secondly, intellectuals were determined to lack confidence about themselves and feared making mistakes. Third, intellectuals might consider they lacked political knowledge or necessary information. Or, lastly, intellectuals were found to be simply uninterested in politics.

Many intellectuals considered thought reform wasn't necessary. One professor explained:

When the Communist's ascended to power in 1949, many progressive intellectuals who had been against Jiang Jieshi and the Nationalists, were eager to join forces with the Communists and were willing to spend time and energy supporting the new regime.

Reassigned to new institutions, some professors found they had so much political work to do, there was not much time for teaching or research. Generally speaking, a school's Communist Party leaders organized faculty members into study groups, and, every day they held discussions from morning until night. During the whole summer of 1953, for example, there was a campaign to criticize the Communist writer Hu Feng, in order to eradicate his influence as a bad intellectual element.

Every morning and afternoon, Party members led faculty to discuss Hu Feng's erroneous ideology. Intellectuals were strongly encouraged to say what they thought and later these "thoughts" were recorded into an individual intellectual's dossier. There was no use sitting quietly, everyone had to participate. Failure to present one's views was considered a sign of opposition, not agreement."[57]

Explaining the difference between leadership's and intellectual's points of view, one intellectual offered: "If you were a communist leader, you are leading socialism, you also do investigations to understand society then decide what things are needed in society. However, to intellectuals, thought reform had the greatest influence.[58]

Soon after the close of the Thought Reform Movement, Chen Ren Bing wrote, "universities realigned on a national scale. The main thing in the reshuffling was the merging and reorganization of Christian schools.[59] "I was transferred to Fudan University's History Department."[60]

Even those intellectuals who remained skeptical accepted transfers to other institutions in 1952 when the Chinese educational system was revamped. Private colleges and universities were closed, as were all departments of psychology, sociology, anthropology and other social sciences. Faculty members were assigned to other state institutions and new departments. A professor's salary was not affected by moving from one university or institution to another.

Chen Renbing felt that the situation did not influence Chinese intellectuals very much, because they were professors at one school and still professors at the other. Reshuffling intellectuals could not have been done easily prior to the Thought Reform Movement. Nor could eliminating courses like sociology and psychology been achieved, without convincing teachers to adopt a very dedicated ideology to serve the people.

> "In the time of the Nationalist corruption there were a lot of colleges, a lot of private colleges. Well, in 1951, all the private colleges added certain conditions. For example, some subjects at Shanghai Normal University, were moved to Fudan and some were moved to East China Normal University. This situation did not influence Chinese intellectuals very much, because they were professors at one school and remained professors. Some thought of educational reform as reorganization meant to centralize management."[61]

The educational reorganization plan affected universities in Beijing. Harvard-trained Historian Chen Daisun explained:

> I think the question of educational reorganization was brought up fully 1 year before implementation. The question was put to universities in Beijing for discussion and by 1952 we agreed that it was better to reorganize. The decision was made from above but after full consultation. In Beijing it involved four universities, Furen, a small college and Qinghua, Beijing, and Yenching Universities. There was no opposition to it. It was not a sudden decision and by 1952 more than 100 residences were prepared as well as recitation halls. At Yenching there was a lot of old housing and at Qinghua there was no problem because not many people went in. The problem was at Beijing University to accommodate more people. The transition was very smooth, except now Qinghua thinks being a technical college has its disadvantages. After 1952, there was no economics department at Qinghua.[62]

After 1949, all sociology departments in the country were beginning to be removed from college curriculums.

> "The Communist government felt that China did not need those bourgeois courses. Except for foreign languages, most of the disciplines in social sciences were not well developed after 1952. Academics in those fields suffered quite a lot. I was transferred to Political Science because for some reason, never explained, sociology had suddenly disappeared from the horizon.[63]

"Sociologists thought dropping sociology[64] was bad. Sociologists originally were fewer anyway. I thought that in Soviet Russia sociology was considered bourgeois. "Sociology studies society. It doesn't matter if you are socialist or capitalist, all have social problems. Some people feel that sociology is all bourgeois, that this type of subject is capitalist. Therefore, they did not study it from then on.[65]

Trying to return to China from the United States during the McCarthy era was uncomfortable but did not deter patriotic Chinese from returning to their motherland. The intellectuals ironic fate in China was to be distrusted for having been in the United States. This is the tragedy of the twentieth century Chinese intellectual. The new government initially treated people like Chen Renbing with respect because many had supported the revolution and were important to the country. Scholars went along with subsequent reorganization of the Chinese educational system and a nationwide socialist re-education campaigns held in the first few years of Mao's rule.

> In China, it is easiest for intellectuals to speak out. Intellectuals have their own ideology and opinions. Intellectuals see a little deeper, wider and more. They read books and have knowledge but still do not have (practical) education. Working people, peasants do not have photographic vision and are naive. They see here and now and don't worry about the future. So, you can say after 1957, China had a period, especially after the cultural revolution, when there was nothing. This is a bad phenomenon. To China and its people, it is bad and abnormal. Normal should be every person able to say whatever they think. But, in reality, while you're saying "good, good" on the outside, your inner feeling is unhappy.[66]

Responding to a call from Mao to speak out for party reform, intellectuals gave critical opinions freely in newspapers and speeches. Mao was unprepared for the vigorous dissent and the wide-ranging topics of criticism surprised party leaders. Several hundred thousand intellectuals were targeted in 1957 purges.[67]

Endnotes

1.   Christian Science Monitor article, Monday March 26, 1984 *Xie Xide-the gentle president of China's Fudan University.*
2.   Interview with Ma Geshun at his home 1992/6/10.
3.   The only occasion that Chen Renbing shook Mao's hand.
4.   Chen Renbing unpublished biography
5.   Dewey, John. (1916) Democracy and Education. The Macmillian Company: New York, pp. 266-67.
6.   Chinese Education since 1949, Chen, Theodore H.E. 1981 Academic and Revolutionary Models Pergamon Press NY, p. 4
7.   In a speech at Qinghua Preparatory College
8.   Interview with Ma Geshun at his home 1992/6/10.
9.   Barry Keenan in The Dewey Experiment in China: Educational Reform and Political Power in the Early Republic p. 141, 151
10.   During the whole summer of 1953, for example, there was a campaign to criticize the Communist writer Hu Feng, in order to eradicate his influence as a bad intellectual element.
11.   Chen, Theodore H.E. (1960)Thought Reform of the Chinese Intellectuals
12.   Chen, Theodore H.E. (1960) Thought Reform of the Chinese Intellectuals Hong Kong University Press, p. 64

13.   Chen said of the Marshall, "His name was often mentioned in the same breath with that of Deng Xiaoping, who was political commissioner. We say "The Grand Army of Liu and Deng."

14.   Other invited guests were Professor Hu Xiaoshi of Central University, Professor Tao Menghe of the Institute for Social Research and President Wu Yifang of Ginling Girl's College.

15.   Hu was accused of surrendering to the bourgeoisie when he supported the Nationalist government that wielded dictatorial power and "suppressed the emergence of new and vital forces." Mistakes were not of a few individuals but of everyone, Hu charged, but he held certain officials responsible saying that "scholasticizing Marx" and mystifying of Marxism makes it a monopoly of only a few.

16.   Chen calls the congress "bogus" because the communist party was purposefully denied participation.

17.   Professor Tao Menghe

18.   Chen Renbing unpublished biography.

19.   Chen noted some of Mao's introductory remarks and who was present at the meeting. "We numbered about ninety. Upon entering the hall, Mao shook hands with each one of us, looking down into each face with a smile. (He was very tall) That was only a few days before he proclaimed the establishment of the People's Republic. For some of those present, Mao said a few pleasant words. To Fei Xiaotong he said, "Your brothers are Fei Chingtong (lawyer) and Fei Chengtong (overseas worker). All three brothers are doing excellent work for the people." To Dr. Ceng Chaolun (1899-1976) grandson of Viceroy Ceng Guofan, Mao said smilingly, "Your native town is Hsiang Hsiang, while my native town is Hsiang Tan, so we are both Hsiang, eh?" Ceng Chaolun, himself a MIT Ph.D. in Chemistry, President of the China Chemical Society was Vice Minister of Higher Education when he was capped a rightist in 1957, eight years after this meeting. When he shook Professor Kwan Mongchueh's hand, Mao said, "When I was in Yenan, I often read your essays in the Xian Chin Feng Ri Bao." With everyone seated in two circles of sofas, Mao poured tea for two old men, Chang Lan on his right and Shan Shengchun on his left, and began to talk."

20.   Chen Renbing unpublished biography.

21.   Chinese Education since 1949 Chen, Theodore H.E. 1981 Academic and Revolutionary Models Pergamon Press NY, p. 1

22.   Fairbanks 360

23.   Li, Moying (1990) Hu Shi and His Deweyan Reconstruction of Chinese History. Unpublished dissertation, Boston University p. 3

24.   Li Moying analyzes the 1917-1937 published works of Hu Shi towards better understanding that generation

25.   according to Professor Tao Shaoyuan

26.   Interview with Tao Shao Yuan Foreign Guest House Shanghai Teacher's University Shanghai July 1992. Professor Tao graduated from the University of Chicago 1925

27.   Interview with Tao Shao Yuan Foreign Guest House Shanghai Teacher's University Shanghai July 1992.

28.   Chen Renbing notes: Mr. Han Shu Tze chief judge of the People's Supreme Court of Shanghai, was appointed Chief Judge "Perhaps Chief Judge Han Shu Tze's path was not very smooth, for later in 1957, he was branded a rightist and deposed."

29.   Chen Renbing unpublished autobiography

30.   Chen explained "On the national level, the Political Consultative Council was being organized on behalf of the Communist Party, other democratic parties, representative groups of the people, the People's Liberation Army, regional representatives as well as overseas Chinese representatives. This new Council was different from the one convened (and destroyed) by the Nationalists, because it shouldered the responsibility of organizing the new government. The Council opened on September 21, 1949 and passed its Common Program, a tentative constitution on September 29."

31.   Chen Renbing unpublished biography. "I was elected as delegate to the National Convention of the League in October 1949, and was elected a member of the League Central Executive Committee. Some of the Committee had been previously elected at a meeting sometime before liberation and I was elected as one of the supplementary members. At this convention Chang Lan was elected Chairman and Shen Chenju vice-chairman."

32.   Chen Renbing unpublished biography.

33.   Chen explained: "In order to avoid trial investigative oversights, a committee including Mr. Wang Yungsheng, publisher and editor of the Ta Kung Pao L'impartialle, Mr. Yong Yiren, former capitalist flour mill owner and Mr. Jiang Yong, well known jurist and former Minister of Justice under the military lord government, and I were appointed."

34.   Chen Renbing unpublished biography.

35.   Fredric J. Spar (1980)

36.   Spar 1980

37.   Chinese statesman Liang Qiqiao reported.

38.   Barry Keenan in The Dewey Experiment in China: Educational Reform and Political Power in the Early Republic p. 142

39.   According to Theodore H.E. Chen, Ch'en Ho-chin (Chen Hoqin) was another personalized target of the Communist party in 1951. Professor Ch'en was a Columbia University Teacher College graduate who studied childhood education.

40.   The Beijing newspaper, The Peoples Daily published a series of ten scathing articles in one month including an editorial by Ho Lin on January 19, 1955.

41.   Chen, Theodore H.E. in (1960) Thought Reform of the Chinese Intellectuals, Hong Kong University Press, p. 49, 84

42.   Chen Renbing unpublished biography. Mr. Chang Lan, one of the six vice-chairman at the same convention. Mr. Sheng Chungjun, League vice-chairman was appointed Chief Justice of the Supreme Court. Mr. Zhang Bojun became Minister of Transportation and later on, Dr. Luo Longji was named Minister of Forest Industry

43.   Interview with Lu Yi July 9, 1992

44.   Our Comfort delegation also included business men and women as well as Christian and Buddhist leaders. Bishop Mao of the Shanghai Episcopalian Church participated as did Miss Tang Diyin, owner of the Green Spot Fountain Pen Factory. Miss Tang started as an apprentice and struggles all the way up the ladder to become one of Shanghai's most famous capitalists. Another well-known capitalist delegate, Mr. Hu Ziang from Zhongqing had three daughters in the Volunteer ranks. Ace flyer Chang Gihui's father, Chang Benzhou joined us, as did model

Shangtung farmer Chan Fugui, who, in his native city, had "Prosperity Village" named after him.

45.   Ching Yen and Chao Dan
46.   Interview with Ma Geshun 1992/6/10
47.   Keenan pp. 122-123
48.   Anonymous by request
49.   Chen Ren Bing's commitment to activism was similar to the viewpoint that Roger B. Jeans writes of Chen's contemporary Zhang Jumai (Carsun Chung) (1887-1969).
50.   Jeans, Roger B. (Ed.)(1992). *Roads Not Taken.* Westview Press: Boulder CO, p. 63
51.   Mr. Lu Yi, was a young reporter during the war of resistance against Japan and the former editor of the Shanghai News Daily
52.   Interview with Lu Yi Shanghai 1992
53.   Chen Renbing unpublished biography
54.   Chen Renbing unpublished biography.
55.   Interview with Lu Yi, July 9, 1992
56.   Chen Renbing unpublished biography
57.   Interview Anonymous 1992
58.   Interview with Lu Yi July 9, 1992.
59.   Chen explained: "Outstanding examples were Yenching University in Beijing and Ling Lan University in Canton, as well as the Baptist-run University of Shanghai, the University of Nanjing, Hwa Nan Girl's College, Ginling Girl's College, Fuzhou Christian Union University and the Suzhou Methodist University. In the case of St. John's University, the majority of its Liberal Arts staff were merged with Fudan University, while the College of Natural Sciences went into the East China Normal University in Shanghai. St. John's Medical and Aurora University Medical schools formed The Second Medical College of Shanghai. The Engineering Department of St. John's went into Tong Ji University of Shanghai."
60.   Chen elaborated: "Another St. John's colleague, Professor Sze Chipan, graduate of Cambridge also joined Fudan at the same time. Already in the department was Dr. Wang Zaoshi of "Seven Gentleman" fame, a University of Wisconsin graduate."
61.   Interview with Mr. Liu Yi 2:00 P.M. Thursday, July 9, 1992 at his home on Wu Kang Road in Shanghai.
62.   Interview with Chen Daisun at Qinghua University May 17, 1982. About an earlier period, Chen said, "I don't think we made too much progress in the period from 1946 to 1949 because, for example, before the war our library had been a good working library, but after 10 years there were almost no books at all. Our problem was to rebuild the library and we barely caught up in 2 years and again after 1947, progress was stopped because of political turmoil. From 1949 to 1952, not a great deal of progress was made. It was a period of readjustment."
63.   Chen Renbing unpublished biography
64.   Professor Chen Daisun commented on the situation at Qinghua University in 1952 when social science courses were abandoned.
65.   Interview with Chen Daisun May 17, 1982.
66.   Interview with Mr. Liu Yi 2:00 P.M. Thursday July 9, 1992 at his home on Wu Kang Road in Shanghai.
67.   Chen Renbing unpublished biography

Chapter IV: The Downfall of Chen Renbing

MAO ZEDONG LABELS CHEN RENBING "BIG RIGHTIST"

The 1957 Anti-Rightist Movement was the first nationwide assault on intellectuals, a sort of literary inquisition. The movement is frequently referred to as the "One Hundred Flowers Campaign" because Mao Zedong used the slogan, "Let One Hundred Flowers Bloom, Let One Hundred Schools of Thought Contend" to introduce an alleged exercise in free speech encouraging intellectuals to voice their opinions about communist party reforms. During the first 7 years of the People's Republic of China, particularly during organized criticism sessions against individuals targeted by the party, intellectuals seemed to resist indoctrination. Now, as Mao announced a rectification movement within the communist party, intellectuals "bloomed" and "contended freely" unleashing direct and veiled criticism which shocked Mao and the top leadership.

Chen Renbing, not willing to pass an opportunity to express his opinions, was one of the first intellectuals to raise questions about the communist party's leadership style. Chen suggested that at the Shanghai Film Studio the Communist Party "wall dividing artists and Party members be broken down at it's foundation" so as to relinquish the glorified worker, peasant, and soldier brand of socialist realism in film propaganda.[1] Chen wrote,

> The Party already has a problem. Everyone knows what socialist theory is, so why do you think the public is so gullible? They are patriotic to our country and honorable. Do you think they don't know what the basis of patriotism and honor is? Do you want to take 7 years of accomplishments and forget everything? The public gives their opinion to people who make films and they want to take away worker, peasant

and soldier propaganda. Why are films approved by a Party director? Does he think that the people are so stupid? Can he just put on a show and think the people will buy it? Do you think people are naive?

Some of the party members are very above the law. They only think about their style, they don't care about anyone else. They don't want to talk about today's problems; they are high up in the party. The first thing we have to realize is the need to change. I still feel sometimes that some party members change their basic attitude, but it is not something they sincerely want to do. This is only to recognize half the mistake. It is impossible to reform completely if you are not sincere yet, have all the people's trust.

I encouraged them to stop covering up mistakes, saying there is no dishonor in admitting one's faults citing the courage of one intellectual[2] who called on all the party members to 'Take down everything and start at the basics'.

I also will take off the mask and treat myself the same way, see my own mistakes. I will be doubly sincere to recognize my wrongs and correct them. From the start, all of us should emulate the party and study their virtues and moral excellence. At the same time, I only take one part as an example. Aren't higher education curriculum and other areas part of "knock the wall down" work?"[3]

In this last phrase, Chen referred to the decision made during the educational reorganization to exclude sociology, psychology, and other humanistic disciplines from all school curriculums because of their allegedly corrupt bourgeois influence. Chen supported and admired Mao and the communists, yet he saw no contradiction to a commitment for free speech and open access to all learning. Chen did not realize that by the time he wrote these sentiments Mao had reinvented the call for free expression and[4] warned of the existence of "open traps" instead of "hidden traps." Unfortunately for Chen, the warning, hidden or open, was not published until July 1, 1957 in the *People's Daily*.

Nearly 3 weeks earlier, on June 9 Mao addressed[5] more than 1,000 Party cadres and a chosen few leftist professors in Shanghai[6] proclaiming, "In Shanghai, you have "trouble-making rightists like Wang Zaoshi, Lu Yi, Chen Renbing, Peng Wenying and Wu Yi confusing the middle elements. The Rightists' progenitors are Zhang Bochun, Luo Longji and Chang Naichi and Beijing is the Rightists' place of origin."[7] Mao demanded the assembled cadres choose between his revolutionary line and the Rightists' "counter-revolutionary line."[8]

By the time Chen read the published warning he already was capped a rightist by Chairman Mao himself and suddenly experienced stinging public disgrace.

Mao's control of the People's Republic from 1949 to 1956 had given the appearance of open dialogue and respect for the people's input. During the Anti-Rightist Movement, intellectuals were stunned to discover how much they were despised by the communist regime. Mao said, "During the past 7 years, we seemed to have the initiative, but this was at best only half true. The surrender of the reactionaries was a sham, and many of the middle elements surrendered unwillingly."[9] On July 9, 1957, in the speech condemning Chen Renbing Mao encouraged continued criticism of Hu Shi, and explained that "The Rightists are very good teachers by negative example." Mao said that "we advocated 'unity-criticism-unity,' but they would not listen." Mao insisted that the Chinese people should "let the rightists poisonous weeds sprout, then uproot them and plow them under for manure. What is more, the Rightists considered that they were not poisonous weeds but fragrant flowers and that we were poisonous weeds and we, not they, should be uprooted.[10] It just did not occur to them that it was precisely they who should be uprooted."

The Anti-Rightist Movement expanded in a way that revealed how Mao viewed intellectuals as a serious threat and insidious influence. Had the strong opinions of intellectuals and former capitalist been allowed to be voiced without tremendous overreaction by Mao the effect may have strengthened his power.

When the China Democratic League was formed a few years before liberation, it attracted western educated intellectuals and became the largest non-communist party sympathetically referred to as the 'party's little brother.' Members initially believed their views were highly valued by the government and saw themselves as standard bearers of the intellectual tradition. However, they soon found out that dissenters were "painted" as counter-revolutionary, anti-Communist, anti-government enemies of the state. Many thousands of people who gave their opinions were "capped" as "Rightists" and became victims of Anti-Rightist Movement punishments determined by Communist leaders, not by courts of law. Labeled Rightists were constantly harangued through the government controlled media. In June 1957, newspapers openly asked if intellectuals had done any good things or just contributed dirty deals in the old society.

Two Shanghai newspapers, *Wen Hui Bao* and *Jiefang Ribao* (*Liberation Daily*), began a daily campaign of incendiary articles on June 14, 1957 strongly criticizing Chen Renbing for his perceived counter-revolutionary ideas. The scathing reviews continued unabated until the end of August, 1957, attacking Chen for having used the rectification campaign "to disrupt and make chaos." Newspapers echoed Mao's initial tirade against the Rightists, stating that Chen's faulty thinking is compared to that of a Beijing rightist, and Chen's remarks are said to "have the strong smell of gunpowder."[11]

Featured prominently in the articles is the accusation that Chen wanted to "settle old accounts."[12] This derives from what Chen had written concerning four problems within the process of party rectification. Despite the fact that Chen's speech was not intended for public consumption,[13] it was printed[14] in its entirety with the caption: "Chen Renbing Holds A Different Opinion on the Method of the Party's Rectification." A black frame under the caption highlighted Chen's suggestions:

> To encourage each and every basic level unit to "air their views," the original big problem remains the same, how to encourage the masses at different grass root units to smash every die-hard attitude inside each and every nook, especially in not a few spots as yet untouched by political movements.

> I feel these days what I have heard of airing of views, I'm afraid only accounts for one-thousandth, one-ten-thousandth of what it should be. After I heard several contradictions presented at the meeting, I felt very heavy hearted and uncomfortable. In the Western Han Dynasty there was a man called Jia Yi (200BC-168BC). Minister Jia Yi faced the direction of the emperor of that time and wrote a memorial, explaining how to govern the empire. Using today's terminology, what he wrote about all were like today's society's internal contradictory political problems. Jia Yi revealed several ranks of findings, some of bitter crying, some of bitter tears, some engendering deep sighs, still others of irrational feelings. I take what I have heard and also make ranks. I don't dare say there is a certain something which makes people cry bitterly. But at least, things that force us to heave sighs are truly too many."[15]

Chen proposed that in the course of party rectification people certainly should not obliterate the good things of the past. Rather, a few who committed notable mistakes should be chosen for judgment by the masses. These few would serve as examples so as to properly educate and dispose of problems effectively and reasonably.

Perhaps Chen's experience as a judge of counter-revolutionaries in the post-1949 honeymoon allowed him to feel that in the course of investigating shortcomings, right and wrong could be distinguished, and mistakes could be corrected. From this vantage point, Chen suggested that old accounts were not beyond calculating.

Chen stirred up a hornet's nest by suggesting that some party comrades who committed errors covered up their own mistakes. Chen reflected twenty five years later on the reasons why his comments engendered such a backlash.

> What I actually said in my writing, was that in the process of Party rectification, the masses were reluctant to speak their minds because they feared possible acts of retribution from those they criticized; offending people concerned; being accused of looking only at the defects; and,

being considered as someone who was asking to 'clear up old accounts.' I said, at this point, that the clearing up of some old accounts, if any, was not as bad as it sounded, provided it was done for the object of learning from the past and drawing lessons for the future, for instance, concerning problems of social waste.

I think the things in my paper that really triggered the anger and contempt of the authorities was where I stated my view of certain old cadres coming to power in the cities after liberation. They were unquestionably loyal to the Party, I said, but since they came into power, they did not learn much in any one line of the business of government. Their stomachs are full, I continued, but they don't use their minds much. Promotion after promotion, however, will always come their way. I also said other things in the same vein. Since the morning of June 9, 1957, being branded a rightist was a foregone conclusion. The Editor (Zhang Chunqiao—author's note)clearly branded me an audacious dissident.[16]

Chen's blunt and honest appraisal served as rich fodder for his detractors and eventually came to use as symbolic icons in his character assassination both in prose and caricature. Portraying Chen as a vain, skirt-chasing, decadent, one account related:

Chen Renbing's personal life is so sordid that you don't want to know. In a secret room in his apartment, he often put on suggestive American records, had dancing parties and also invited women of loose morals to his apartment. Once, he was at a cigarette stand buying cigarettes and saw a woman clerk. He bought all her stock and brought her to his apartment. When he was teaching at St. John's University, his beady eyes frequently scanned for pretty girls in the class. After class he would invite them to dance and if they refused he would lower their grade.[17]

One article declared how Chen even disregarded directives emanating from Mao's inner circle, including those from Zhang Qunchiao who would become even more powerful as one of the infamous "Gang of Four" during the Cultural Revolution. "Chen Renbing once said, 'Zhang Chunqiao wants to talk with me, but I don't want to talk with him'", the article related. The editorial questioned "What kind of talk is this?" when revealing Chen uttered the phrase "The cards are in our hands. If we speak about them, it will force him to show his hand." The state-controlled media concocted a case against Chen that accused him of wanting to overthrow the government.[18]

Wu Nan[19] in an article published in *Wen Hui Bao*, criticized Chen Renbing for speaking aggressively about the rectification campaign and criticizing the tactics used to implement the campaign and stated that with "various Rightist intellectuals leading the way, the helpful atmosphere of reform is being disrupted and not really according to communist spirit and guidance."[20]

Chen's "ridiculous ideas" are severely criticized as part of his "whole set of confused ideology" which allegedly damaged people's trust in the Communist Party[21] by placing the whole country into turmoil[22] and dishonoring the Democratic League's history

> In the past few years, Chen Renbing often speaks for the cultural world. Every time he sees people or is in political meetings he says he is a cultural type of person and not a political ideologist. When he meets anybody with a problem, he does not have the capacity to investigate the situation well, he just hurries to write some material to the Party and government specializing in hitting and striking. Chen seems to arrange his attacks for revenge. Recently a director happened to hire some actors to replace some others to correct some theater problems. Basically, all that was necessary was just to explain the situation and everything would be okay. But under Chen Renbing's eyes, it was a very serious problem. He had to address the theater reform and even wrote some material and distributed it to the cultural department and central committee.

Chen was accused of wanting to retaliate against the Party. Anti-Chen criticism quoted Liu Shaoqi, one-time heir apparent to Mao who, along with his well-educated wife, had been mercilessly reviled some years earlier. "For persons who have erred, it is easy to punish and expel them. But the problem did not address how such wrong thinking developed. Strict punishment did not ensure the Party would not make the same or even greater mistakes."[23] The article flatly interpreted Chen's phrase 'merely a gentle breeze and mild rain' would not be enough to deal with the problems, intimating that Chen advocated choosing some wrong thinking persons and punishing them.

The inference was that had party rectification been carried out according to Chen's terms it would have failed. Success of the rectification depended on controlling dissenting opinions and free exchange of ideas. Chen's ideas were considered dangerous to the regime as they could easily lead the masses towards the wrong way of punishment. Ironically, the very point Chen tried to make was not to treat people as though they were stupid or naive.

Instead of appreciating Chen's notion of how trusting mass opinion could work for the party's advantage, Chen was characterized for his crestfallen pessimism and accused for not saying anything about the years of achievements for socialist construction. Supposedly, Chen despaired about current conditions when quoting Mao's words, "Modesty helps one to go forward, whereas conceit makes one lag behind" as a warning to some Communist Party members. Party leaders felt Chen had become arrogant and cocky.

Chen, it seemed, did not trust the Party to lead the rectification movement and did not have confidence in the party. Chen was accused of committing serious errors, especially in his position as Democratic League Central Committee Member and Secretary-General of the Democratic League in Shanghai.

Headlines[24] splashed across newspapers revealed the party's perception of Chen's group of rightists as dangerous and vicious. Article after article inferred how, while at St. John's University, Chen wanted the China Democratic League to become the Capitalist Democracy Party and expressed political views meant overthrow the leadership of the Communist Party.[25] Within the ranks of the Shanghai Democratic League some wondered,

> When Mr. Chen Renbing talked of "pitiful reactions between the party and people" and the feeling he is "heavy hearted", it is nonsense! Is China in agony over rectification and life unbearable? Is this caused by the Communist Party? No! The reason Chen is sad seems to be for the people, but lies are lies and cannot be proven without facts. People are happy for new China, are working hard, enjoying the victory of developing socialism. They love and thank the Party. The only exception is Chen Renbing. He holds the standard for a minority group, has nothing to do with workers or peasants. There are problems, but they are not serious, not worth feeling sad about. Chen Renbing told a lie with closed eyes, pounding his chest at the platform, exaggerating the problems. Isn't it propaganda to sow dissension among the party and masses? It is hard for western nations to differentiate. Western news reports that 'mainland Chinese are suffering, they are resisting the government's lead.' Rightists are so welcomed by western countries and powerful people in the so-called free world.[26]

Cartoons ridiculing Chen Renbing, show thousands of angry factory workers surrounding a man crouched under an umbrella inscribed "Rightist" carrying a sheaf of rolled paper in one hand that reads "anti-socialist" while holding a sheet of paper, inscribed "Anti-Party." Workers shout and wave banners "Completely eradicate rightist's outrageousness," "We're against their ridiculous thinking," "Distinguish between right and wrong," and "We've got the correct idea." In the background, a huge banner reads, "Join the anti-rightist struggle." Another caricature illustrates a "rightist" putting on makeup in front of a mirror. The caption reads, "Rightists covering up."[27]

The people against Rightists are portrayed as their non-Communist peers, themselves on the path to establish Socialism. The message the newspapers and media conveyed was that even the Rightists' equals consider them wrong. This argument was further used against one of Chen's friends who argued the concept of 'dang tian xia' "Party Kingdom" had created a monochromatic, one family-empire China. The newly-coined phrase 'Party Kingdom' hurt the Communists.[28]

The Case Against Chen Renbing

One intellectual[29] reflected in retrospect some 30 years later that "the present builders of our country all experienced the same ideological remolding." Therefore, he now considered it acceptable being named a rightist in 1957.[30] Another[31] described the ordeal he shared as a patriotic intellectual capped and punished with Chen Renbing.

> Things happened at that time as I predicted they would happen.[32] Mao Zedong gave the word that to speak out it is not a crime, but, if you had already spoken out, you better be careful. We intellectuals hoped to do a good job, towards a good direction, but they misinterpreted us. They thought we were bad eggs. Chen Renbing and I were both unlucky. Together we were both reeducated in 1958. We went to the countryside to labor. This labor did not scare us, we carried shoulder poles and worked. Do you think the purpose was purely reeducation?
>
> Chen Renbing was a very talented person. He could speak, he was educated and he was very honest and open. We were in the countryside doing labor for half a year. Afterwards we went to an outside supervised area, in the outskirts of Shanghai. They called that place the Socialist Reeducation Center. We two were in the same class, we ate together, we slept together and worked together, studied together and understood each other very well.
>
> At that time it was very unfair. You know in our country the constitution also protects free speech, and Mao himself requested we speak out our opinions. This was a big loss for China because sincerity is very important. But now, some people speak lies and study lies and when they speak out its the same. Talking about problems, they all say lies. Towards progress, we discovered, this had no merit.[33]

Were criticisms in the 1957 anti-rightists campaign a precursor to those during the Cultural Revolution? Intellectuals agree that the decade long cultural revolution was chaotic and uncivilized, yet, in 1957 criticism against rightists was also without reason. Newspapers did not report according to the facts[34] and there were too many people named rightists.[35] Twisted truths not only saddened Chen, they ruined his political and academic careers. One account mistakenly stated that Chen's American sojourn was church funded. (In fact, Chen was proud to say that $1,000.US his father earned from the sale of his book *Echoes From China* was the funding Chen used to begin studies in the United States.) The article continued the character assassination of Chen Renbing:

Chen is the son of a minister. He studied in a church college, after graduation the church sponsored him to study in America. He became addicted to the materialistic and democratic politics of America. He enjoyed being a member of the overseas fraternity organization, Flip Flap.[36] Chen became a Nationalist treasury department assistant, and member of the New Life Movement, Nationalist Party and the Li Zhi She Club. In addition, he designed a flag for the San Qing Tuan.

After the end of the War of Resistance Against Japan, American imperialists barged into China and Chen Renbing was very excited about this. One time he attended a party held by the American ambassador Leighton Stuart. He made a welcome speech in English, he bowed, scrapped and flattered in an attempt to glorify America, but ended up making himself look foolish. He acted to find favor in American eyes and to get official position.

But by this time the Liberation Army's strong forces pinpointed their movement and American imperialism had no way to rescue the Nationalist's counterrevolutionary future. As soon as Chen Renbing saw the movement he knew it was not right, he pretended to be progressive and agreeable to revolution. On one side he joined the progressive magazine[37] becoming main editor, on the other hand he was at St. John's University teaching "Three Principles of the People."[38]

On behalf of the Shanghai Democratic League, Chen wrote about China's movie business and chaired a creativity discussion at the Shanghai movie studios where some Democratic League members were prominent movie and stage directors, and actors. Chen Renbing was criticized for targeting famous singers and actors, proclaiming how much he loved music while flaunting and name-dropping. Chen acknowledged traditional opera performers were well-represented in the Democratic League but too few singers were League members. In 1957, after Chen led five discussion meetings with artists and directors at the Shanghai Film Studio 24 famous directors and screen stars who voiced their sorrows at that forum were branded "rightists."[39] Xin Hua News Agency reporters also exposed the real facts of how Chen Renbing immediately seized the opportunity to initiate a series of five meetings to discuss the Shanghai Film Industry and secretly made a list of dissatisfied intellectuals who would attend the meeting. None of them were Party or League members and they didn't even invite people who were close to the Party.[40]

Chen's speech[41] "To Understand People, to Respect People and to Have Regard for People" was published in the *People's Daily* article on August 17, 1956. A year later, Chen came to learn that this speech also triggered some hatred. Chen argued that before one could really have regard for China's intellectuals, one should understand and truly respect them. Likewise, before one respects intellectuals, one must possess a high appreciation and respect for scientific knowledge. Chen said, "Intellectuals are but the holders and conduits of knowledge, one who fails to respect knowledge is not likely to give high esteem to intellectuals.[42]

Newspaper editorials with bold headlines plagued Chen for the length of the summer of 1957.[43] A score of intellectuals related their own conversations and joined the attack against Chen Renbing.

> After liberation, the Communist Party took care of all the old society's intellectuals and working personnel, those who were professors remain professors, administrators were still invited to remain administrators, from this magnanimous policy, I still don't know where is the place we are owed an apology. Today's backward approach still claims the Communist Party has accounts to be settled. I don't know what purpose this serves, I hope that Chen Renbing will clarify this.[44]

> Fudan University's China Democratic League central committee members, including myself, universally disagree with Chen Renbing's statement which gives people the impression that internally the Communist Party is very rotten, very prejudiced, very chaotic. Chen Renbing is a Democratic League Central Committee member, Shanghai Democratic League officer and comrade leader. I hope he is able to examine the origins of his thinking very well, consider well everyone's opinions, and not hurriedly examine them, because it would be easy to change over also easy to change back.[45]

On June 27, 1957, Chen Renbing gave a self-criticism before Fudan University's entire staff of history department professors. Chen said, "I was influenced very deeply by the old democraticism towards accepting working class leadership. On an intellectual level I could accept it, on an emotional level it was a contradiction. My ideological thinking basically towards the Party leadership has an opposition sentiment. My acting independently and defiantly has increased unscrupulously towards creating my political advantage."[46]

Some charged that Chen's self-criticism was dishonest, remonstrating him to honestly, frankly and remorsefully confess. Opinions expressed were that Chen was a tricky, unscrupulous person who cares not for the interests of the people but for advancing his own position. Supposedly these negative opinions demoralized Chen to the point where "Chen Renbing did not know whether to laugh or cry."[47] Another professor sought to expose Chen's true motives when he described how Chen Renbing rushed to Nanjing to wantonly take part in Democratic League liaison activities when liberation was imminent. Later, however, when Chen realized that Nanjing would not replace Beijing as the capital of China, and he would not be in the limelight, he abandoned his post as part of the group preparing to welcome the Liberation Army.

GANG OF FOUR MEMBER ZHANG QUNCHIAO CRITICIZES CHEN RENBING

Threads connecting the Anti-Rightist Campaign and the Cultural Revolution were finally revealed after many years. Chen Renbing always wondered who authored the libelous July 14, 1957 article insinuating he was a spokesman of the imperial, feudal Nationalist bureaucracy. That article sealed his fate. It represented the antithesis of how Chen considered himself a well known fugitive from the Nationalist reign of terror.[48] The riddle was solved when the New Literature Publication Association of Shanghai printed *Today's Collection's,* by Zhang Chunqiao. Chen referred to Zhang as "the Number One Brain and Chief of Staff of the Gang of Four" who promulgated 10 years of disaster known as The Great Proletarian Cultural Revolution.

Chen surmised Zhang Chunqiao began to win Mao's favor by the number of intellectuals he netted and victimized in 1957 and 1958. Another Gang of Four member, Yao Wenyuan was also active in the right-ist purge.[49] Zhang employed the pseudonym[50] Wu Song in attacks which signaled what was to follow in the Cultural Revolution from 1966-1976.[51] Wu Song wrote:

> Chen Renbing's intentional confusing of the issues greatly angers all present. They accuse Chen of making a 'lax self-examination' because Chen only admitted that 'he and Luo Longji and others had a small club, but since last year, didn't have any activities.' When he said that in the meeting, everyone suddenly groaned, everyone says he's a liar. We want Chen Renbing to answer, what kind of tricks does this little club have? Do you use international anti-communism as propaganda? People continue to ask 'Who is supporting Chen Renbing?'[52]

A regular feature, "ALL THE RIGHTISTS' FACES", began appearing daily for a few weeks in the *Liberation Daily*. The bold-faced print high-lighted anti-Rightist's articles, and the heading was illustrated with humor-ous drawings of intellectuals as buffoons.[53] A cartoon caricature, resem-bling Chen Renbing, shows him standing on a music record, with a dollar sign emblazoned on his heart, while he carries a "fan the flame" torch in his hand.[54]

Another article[55] stated: 'No matter what his words and feeling, Chen Renbing is an anti-Party careerist, and a comprador bourgeois whose will is very strong, the same as Luo Longji. Chen has said he hated veteran cadres.'

> Something was very strange about Chen before and after liberation. Chen Renbing was involved in some democratic movements, ran the *Outlook* magazine, and edited *China Reconstructs*. He seemed to be

progressive, but it was only a surface phenomenon for him, it was not his nature. His nature was Anti-Party, Anti-Soviet.

Chen Renbing knew how to do his political speculation and he had a series of techniques and a scheme for confusing tricks. In 1945, he joined the Democratic League. He was appreciated by Luo Longji and Luo recommended him as a central committee member of the Democratic League. Chen communicated with Luo by mail and telegram, to plan various anti-party actions. After liberation, Luo coined the fallacy of "one way line and several strong points." Luo took the relationship between Party and various democratic parties, as several different fortified points on a one-way line, rather than the relationship of leadership and followers.

Chen wrote some articles, made speeches to spread this kind of view and opposed the Party. Chen also led his organization with Peng Wenyin. He had no regard for the instruction from the central committee of the Democratic League, stopping it from expanding membership, and developing the members. At first, he wanted to strengthen their strong point to get the organization at Shanghai. Next, he used the Democratic League to carry out anti-party action.

Before 1952, the anti-party organization led by Chen and Peng often met. They took the Qinghua University circles as a strong point and organized the Party to draw some of the masses, and opposed the branch of the Eastern Democratic League. Chen's trusted followers also said not to be a 'gray grandson of the Communist Party.' How vicious he was! They took the comrades who drew close to the Party, to be 'gray grandsons of the Party.' Were being fine sons and daughters of the party not glorious?

He distorted the Party policy toward intellectuals and overestimated the intellectual's progress. It seemed that the intellectuals were not to be remolded. He considered the main problem was how the Party used them, not knowing the characteristic of intellectuals and not respecting them. Then, he criticized in an article to the *Liberation Daily*, "To Understand People, To Respect People, To Have Regard for People." He considered the problem was that the Party didn't esteem people.

At some forums managed by Chen, he continued to spread his view, he often said to the masses that 'we really understand the intellectuals,' 'the Democratic League was a warm family for intellectuals,' and the 'Democratic League should represent the benefits of intellectuals.' He used these kinds of words to confuse the masses' thinking. He also was a League secretary and used his position to visit, to investigate some famous movie producers, directors and doctors so as to separate the relationship between the Party and the masses, and to lead these people to an anti-Party path.

Not only older intellectual were targeted as rightists. Serious repercussions awaited students when reports surfaced[56] that, "a group of undergraduates from the National University of Beijing was reported to have criticized the ideology of Mao and told a large audience that "Marxism had ceased to develop as an ideology ever since 1895" while Mr. Mao's thought was still in a metamorphic process between metaphysics and dialectics. "Dictatorship of the proletariat is the root of evils. Suppression of counter-revolutionaries yielded no result whatever. Capitalized democracy is better than socialism, let's take up the revolutionary tradition of the May Fourth Movement.'"[57] By espousing the ideals of the May Fourth Movement, students were making a ubiquitous inference to the importance of the ideology of May Fourth leader Hu Shi. This was blasphemy to the party hierarchy and signaled the intellectual's mutiny was spreading.

Party leaders were further enraged with a plan for improving scientific research drawn up for the Central Committee of the China Democratic League. The directive urged that scientists should be freed from administrative work, given the leisure, freedom and funds necessary for free individual study and relieved of the close guidance and controls that hampered their efforts. The proposals said "the security system now in force is too strict and too inflexible and should be improved."[58] "The memorandum objected to the present attitude of rejecting the social sciences, asserting that this had reached the extent of 'regarding state policies and measures of government as objective laws of society and paying little attention to investigations and research as well as the laws of objective factors.'"[59] Mao countered his "attackers" by leading his own vitriolic criticism of anti-party views.

On June 8, 1957, Mao Zedong published an inner-Party directive for the Central Committee of the Chinese Communist Party entitled, Muster Our Forces To Repulse The Rightists Wild Attacks.[60] Mao wrote, "Call meetings of the principal cadres and veteran workers and explain to them that some bad capitalists, bad intellectuals and reactionary elements in society are mounting wild attacks against the working class and the Communist Party in an attempt to overthrow the state power. They should make sure not to be taken in by these persons. Stop anyone trying to incite the people."[61]

On July 1, 1957, Hong Kong newspapers reported that "Communist China accused timber industry minister Luo Longji and communications minister Zhang Bojun of having plotted to overthrow the Communist party, but indicated they would not be punished. Both are members of the Democratic League."[62] The league assailed them as being too enthusiastically critical of the regime after Mr. Mao invited open discussions of internal 'contradictions'. The charges were announced in *The People's Daily*, the official Communist newspaper, in an editorial denunciation of 'rightist' criticism."[63]

Chen capitulated and partially admitted his anti-party activities. During a Fudan University Democratic League rectification meeting when referring to his discussions about film, Beijing opera, local opera, literature, publishing and traditional Chinese painting,[64] Chen admitted, "I am a Rightist and the ringleader of Luo Longji's clique in Shanghai. "Since 1956, I have not had contact with Luo Longji." Chen explained how "Luo Longji's clique had several guiding principles.

> First, unite several small cliques who put their own benefits over the people's interests, go into the internal levels of the League to usurp position and power. Secondly, openly or secretly anti-Soviet, be against progressive comrades who tend to be close to the Party. Third, only orally endorse socialism, and, in reality from the standpoint of the reactionary class, towards new things, new institutions, towards social-ist reforms, adopt a revisionist attitude.[65]

Chen used the standard method of contrition, known as 'self-criticism', yet the editorials said "people still weren't satisfied with his attitude, want-ing him to continue thoroughly justifying himself."[66] A reporter highlight-ed what he deemed were 'despicable methods' Chen used to recruit mem-bers to the Democratic League. "Chen Renbing often said: "So long as we can win over several public figures in some work units we will control the situation." In order to capture the famous figures, by hook or by crook, Chen would pay somebody a visit, invite someone to dinner, send a car or, go as far as to allow the new member not to take an oath, not to write a resume, not participate in meetings as bait to induce them to join."[67]

Other condemned rightist tried to support the outspoken Chen Renbing yet cautioned him for his behavior. A Chinese traditional painter, who had been relegated to the category of "Stubborn Rightists" wrote to Chen, "If there is unexpected praise, or unattainable demands for perfec-tion, remain unperturbed. Never surrender your ideals to hatchet men. If your opinion on public affairs is from the bottom of your heart, then you have to believe in yourself, don't be afraid of anything, advocate and per-severe to the end, you no longer need to do self-criticism." Chen did incriminate himself further "thoroughly unmasking himself" in what mod-ern day readers will see as a heart-breaking surrender to the bullies who broke his resolve.[68]

> After he spoke about many things, Chen Renbing again gave more self criticism saying:[69] I owe too much to the people. I even had the effron-tery to make wild arrogant presumptions, raising a hue and cry about settling old accounts. What I owe the Party and the people is so heavy, I can't even carry on.
>
> I'm coming back to raise a hue and cry, simply I return good for evil, I am ungrateful, I've stood for landlordism and imperialism. As a con-temptible rightist, my "patriotism" has a big problem, it's fake,

because I'm standing on anti-Party position, anti-socialism and counterrevolutionary standpoint, definitely, I have problems. I'm very sure
I have a problem knowing if I stand with friend or foe.

In 1952, during Thought Reform, I was at St. John's University and
made a false statement to Party member named Cui Yi. I said in 1950
my daughter was sent by her mother from Singapore to America without my permission. In fact, on October 12, 1950, in response to her letter, I gave my permission. After 2 weeks, I went to Shanghai to attend
a meeting. I even made a big speech, supporting the Anti-American
movement. Looking at myself, I should be ashamed about having two-
faces. I deceived the Party, yet afterwards, I still went to North Korea
to entertain troops. Besides that, in the case of Huang Longhua, I supported changing his death sentence into a life sentence. My cousin was
a member of the Zhong Tong spy organization of the Nationalists
arrested after liberation. I attempted to shelter him.

Today I reveal our little clique's intentions, methods, and the course of
our major criminal activities. Our main intention is to, within cultural
education and other aspects to create and exaggerate dissatisfaction
towards the Party, to separate the intellectuals from the Party, in this
way take away the Party leadership, then we would take over. This is
what kind of ugly face we have toward reaching our goal. Now I hate
this kind of criminal clique, I also hate myself deeply, I'm very deeply
disappointed in myself since the Party and the people have shown me
kindness and moral support, I ask the Party to give me the most severe
punishment. I implore the Party to give me another chance to begin my
life anew. I want to thoroughly reform myself, walk the path of
Socialism.

From now I will be very sincere in accepting the Party leaders guidance,
I won't be of two minds anymore.[70]

Chen admitted that the "leading lights among the Rightists" were "now
attacking all Communist theory and policy as dogma." The two non-
Communist leaders[71] used the recently proclaimed "free contention" policy of the Communist leadership as a cover under which to incite dissatisfaction among intellectuals, create disturbances, scoff at the successes of
the Communist party and exaggerate every little fault, undermining
Chinese-Soviet friendship and used two newspapers, the *Guangming Daily
News* in Beijing (the official organ of the China Democratic League) and
the *Wen Hui Bao* of Shanghai to further their campaigns.[72]

Reporting that "they would not be punished and that it would be
enough to brand them as Rightists, the *People's Daily* added "bourgeois
and reactionary forces had been deliberately left unchecked in order to let
the masses understand how dangerous they are and participate in their
total elimination. We organized a trap to catch all those who were planning

to usurp power."[73] Photos of Dr. Luo Longji and Mr. Zhang Bochun high-light "Beijing Reports New Confessions—Two Non-Communist Leaders Said to have Conceded Activity Against Reds."

> Luo and Zhang have made sweeping and abject confessions of anti-Communist activity at the closing session of the Chinese Communist National People's Congress.[74]

Dr. Luo Longji was summarily removed from his Timber industry post. He was also removed as vice-chairman of the China Democratic League, as member of the Political Consultative Conference and as deputy to the National People's Conference from his native province.[75] For his critical opinions, Mr. Zhang Bojun was stripped of his government position, removed as chief of the *Guangming Daily*, removed as vice-chairman of the Democratic League and of the Political Consultative Conference, removed as deputy to the National People's Congress from his native province and from the chairmanship of his own political party, the China Peasants and Workers Democratic Party.[76]

As for Mr. Chu Anping, besides confessing his mistakes made in his "Party-Kingdom" article, he was removed from his positions as editor-in-chief of the *Guangming Daily*, as deputy chief of the Propaganda Department of the September Third Party, and, as deputy to the National People's Congress from his native Jiangsu Province.[77]

THE RIGHTIST STIGMA—CHEN'S CIRCLE

Chen Renbing explained the devastating impact political shocks had on families of rightists.

> Once capped a "rightist", there followed endless meetings in which you were criticized, reprimanded and remonstrated by those leftist gen-tlemen in your outfit. It seemed they were always correct, according to classical standards, and you were required to make endless self-incrim-inations and confessions, expressing your determination to reform your thought and try to begin life as a new man, never again to doubt the Party leadership.

> The fact was, in the process of deciding who should be capped, persons who happened to have expressed displeasure at a single Party member, even for justifiable reasons, were likely to be looked upon as an Anti-Party elements.[78] Six Beijing University Professors were earmarked "rightists" because they submitted a plan for reforming higher educa-tion.[79]

> In the case of older people, they might be fired from jobs and made to do light labor. In my case, I had one third of my salary cut, and my

professional title wiped off. There were many "rightists" who had a larger part of their income cut off, and sent away to do sundry labors.[80]

My father was branded rightist. I never did find out the reason why, in the vocabulary of the *People's Daily*, father was named a "bourgeois rightist." Born a carpenter's son and living most of his life as a poor teacher, it was absurd to call him a "capitalist rightist." My father was a patriot who held his patriotism as high as his devotion to God. He wrote an article for the *People's Daily* entitled "To Love My Country And My Church At The Same Time." I am sure the leftist dogmatists hated this sort of thing bitterly, and thought father a heretic. Once, in the *People's Daily*, he had written, "I hold those who desecrate churches as persons destroying my ancestral tombs." Father thought Party policies toward religion were correct and he approved of them. He admired Mao Zedong and gave him credit for restoring China's independence and freedom and beating down corrupt rule.

Father simply adored Premier Zhou Enlai. The treatment father received was such an unexpected blow for an old man. He never recovered from the shock and sorrow and died in 1963. It was a blessing that he was not to witness the Great Proletarian Cultural Revolution of 1966, which would have rained blows upon him many times more terrible.

I was capped on June 14 and a series of criticism and self-criticism meetings followed. I made a number of "confessions." Other "rightists" were going through the same mill, making nauseating self-incriminating statements, while the newspapers reveled in slander, rumors, and baseless stories, all hearsay trumpeted across the pages.[81]

When the social status of a rightist was found to be bourgeois, it was then determined whether to make him or her a BIG rightist. All those who went abroad were targeted. Now these people have become backbones of our country. It is too bad that they suffered from the Anti-Rightist Movement of 1957. This kind of story may be multiplied how many times? I don't know. Between 1957 and 1983, I was allowed to do just about 4 years of University classroom teaching.[82]

From September 15 until December 31, 1958, 48 rightists from the Shanghai area, 45 men and 3 women, including Chen Renbing, were encamped in a suburban farm house.[83] The intellectuals were divided into four groups of 12[84] digging the soil or harvesting in the morning and, in the afternoons and evenings, studying their 'anti-Party' and 'anti-people guilt.'[85] Beginning in February 1958, the group was sent to join the College of Socialism in Jiadin, Shanghai. There, the routine was the same, labor in the morning and discussion sessions, in the afternoons and evenings.

'Graduated' on a July day, Chen Renbing checked into the hospital weighing 150 pounds and was hospitalized for 4 months with acute heart disease. Chen was released in November weighing a mere 104 pounds.

> "Around age 50, Dr. Chen began to have heart problems, in part due to all his political troubles. When "Rightists" were sent to the countryside for reform through labor, some of his family members told me that Dr. Chen went barefoot into the rice fields, where there were leeches. He got a bad case of "Hong Kong Feet" which infected his heart and he suffered a high fever and intestinal inflammation. No medicine would lower the fever. Afterwards, he went in and out of four hospitals and doctors finally discovered that he had gotten heart disease from the leeches in the field. Dr. Chen was treated with double dosages of antibiotics, four needles at a time, day and night. In this manner, his fever dissipated. The treatment continued for a few weeks and he lost so much weight he looked like skin and bones. His heart was permanently damaged.[86]

Chen passed his 50th birthday in the hospital during the Moon Festival of 1959. From Beijing, he received a hand-written poem from his father. "Our son's 50th birthday makes his parents feel old indeed." Marcus wrote, adding that it was God's blessing which made it possible since his son had traveled over uneven roadways. Because Renbing was credulous, he was cheated and victimized. Marcus hoped his eldest son would learn from the past and endeavor to concentrate more in one field of study and serve the people.

Chen Renbing was impressed with the note and commented,

> Very noticeable was a clause that hoped I would make special effort to win membership in the Communist Party, because, as a "rightist" in the same boat as me, he felt it would be good for me. I think father was sincere in his aspirations for his seriously ailing son, in a sickbed far away in Shanghai. The poem showed the kind of feeling father had for the Communist Party. He sincerely wished the Party well, even though he was treated so shamefully. In 1980, father's case was rectified by the Party Central and in 1981, at the National Convention of Christian Organizations, his name was restored to honor and he was merited as among the founders of the new Christian cause.

> In retrospect, the Anti-Rightist Movement, in it's vastly expanded form, did enormous damage to the trust intellectuals had in the Communist Party. Their confidence was betrayed. Men like my father, who always had defended the Party's policies, felt deeply hurt. Nevertheless, father was loyal to the cause of the Party and to men like Zhou Enlai to the end.

> The Anti-Rightist Movement has left social consequences more profound that most things in recent Chinese history. Tens of thousands of

intellectuals made "confessions" of things they did not do and words they did not say. They lied against themselves, something forbidden by traditional Chinese ethics.

The Chinese are a moral race. Honesty to oneself was the supreme standard for traditional scholars. To force such a multitude to such debasement was terrible. It was lucky that most, perhaps 99% of the "rightists" have, as of 1981, been rectified. That is, their verdict been declared false and void. This proved that the vast volume of self-incriminations were lies told out of necessity.

This, I think, is a serious lesson for this generation and many generations to come. Moral principals are not to be trifled with, not even for political necessity. I for one, have been guilty of writing false "confessions".

The Anti-Rightist Movement wasted manpower, wasted brains and wasted social wealth, which a developing country like China could ill afford. From 1957 to 1958, when most "rightists" were capped, until people were rectified and placed back in their original positions, nearly a quarter of a century had slipped away. Many people died from doing heavy labor or from malnutrition or lack of medical care.

China has suffered as a result of the Anti-Rightist Campaign in the realm of democratic progress and human rights. China had adopted a Constitution in 1954. It was a progressive document, guaranteeing citizen's rights of speech and expression. Judicial powers were vested in proper courts and prosecutors offices. In criminal cases and in the treatment of underage delinquents, there were due procedures for placing truly guilty persons in labor camps, after constitutional processes of trial and formal decisions in accordance with the law. To send a man, untried and outside the orbit of a judicial set-up, to a remote place of labor, retarded China's progress.[87]

AFTERMATH OF THE ANTI-RIGHTIST MOVEMENT

The *Liberation Daily* of September 16, 1959 reported "According to the Shanghai Chinese Communist Party Central Committee, a decision has been made recently to remove caps from one group of reformed intellectuals including Chen Renbing[88] and in all, 2,062 people.[89] On December 12, 1960, the *Liberation Daily* announced[90] that rightist caps were removed from another group of reformed Shanghai intellectuals revealing that the scope of the Anti-Rightist Movement was greatly expanded to the point where most cases were determined to have been wrongly judged in the first place.

In June 1980, five intellectuals "never capped wrongly on national central level", rectified but correctly accused are: Zhang Bojun, Luo Longji, Chu Anping, Chen Renbing and Peng Wenying. Chen Renbing outlived them all and in a February 27, 1982 interview, Dr. Chen Renbing said "of the 22 rightists declared wrongly capped, a decision was made that five members of Democratic Parties, the China Democratic League and the September Third Party, were to be kept as bone fide rightists".

> Today, we are witnessing a democratic comeback. Perhaps the greatest teaching is the sad experience of the 1957 Movement's damage. This might be a case of what Mao used to say, 'turning a bad thing into something good'. What a price for the lesson. The human cost, probably half a million souls and their families, in a 25-year span. I tremble to think of the magnitude of such an equation. It is well worth pondering.

> The government declared 99% of "rightists" were wrongly capped, but I was not wrongly capped in 1957. They told me 'What was done was a correct act, so your case is not to be rectified, your branding was correct.' "According to their rule, I was not supposed to get my old salary and title back. But they made an exception to their own rule, but, with no explanation. They said nothing, I said nothing because I knew I would be wasting my breath.

> I know rightists were branded at different levels. Those of us who were appointed to the central committee, this crowd, had their branding done by the central committee itself. All decisions came from Beijing as whether to be rectified or not. At the end of May, 1980, a confidential document, published by three Hong Kong newspapers, announced that 5 rightists were not to be rectified, and that 22 more who were released, were determined to have been wrongly capped.[91]

Heavy Hearted 1957 breaks free from many years of reticence, making it the first narrative literature report of the Anti-Rightists Struggle published in China. The author, Ye Yonglie, narrates the unfortunate life of eight "big rightists" who were "well known" at home. The 400,000 character essay describes the panorama of the Anti-Rightists Movement.[92]

Ye writes, "1957 is a heavy-hearted page in modern Chinese history. Li Weihan,[93] then head of the United Front, vice-chairman of the National Assembly, vice-chairman of the Chinese People's Political Consultative Conference, and central committee member of the Communist Party recollected the earthshaking anti-rightist struggle. In 1984, when he was about to leave this world, he wrote the book *Recollections and Considerations* and spoke of 1957:

> At the time I was head of the United Front Committee, towards the Anti-Rightist I was very aggressive, and I am responsible for making

lots of mistakes. Today I still feel deeply guilty and responsible for mis-
judging my comrades and friends.

The result of the anti-rightist struggle is very severe, taking one huge
group of intellectuals and patriotic people and Communist Party
cadres and mistakenly labeling them anti-rightists, making their families suffer for a long period of time, constantly attacking, torturing.
They couldn't use their intelligence and knowledge toward helping the
country build socialism. This is not only their misfortune, but the country's misfortune as well. In the whole country more than 550,000 rightists were capped. Among them, quite a few were intellectual specialists
and experienced business managers and industrialists. Fifty percent of
them lost their government jobs. Quite a few among them were forced
to reform through labor, some of them lost everything, their family and
home. The minority stayed at their original workplace, most were misplaced and wasted their talents."

On November 11, 1984, 88-year old Li Weihan died in Beijing. The
commendable former leader of the United Front Committee, before he
died, left behind the writings and impression that thoroughly understood that people need to wake up and see mistakes.

We need to know that in 1957 he was the important organizer of the
Anti-Rightist Struggle, it was not an easy thing for him to so honestly
and frankly admit he himself was wrong. Additionally, in his later
years nearly every month he received hundreds of letters urging him to
speak up for people victimized and wrongly accused by the party. Most
of these people were prospective members of the United Front
Committee. Li Weihan sincerely took care of the letters one by one,
regardless of his age and illness, doing the best he could to speak up for
those people falsely accused and who cruelly suffered for his mistakes.

On May 16, 1966, the Cultural Revolution officially began, however, roots
were first planted on June 8, 1957 when the Anti-Rightist Struggle developed and elevated leftist ideology and expanded it to a new condition.
During the Cultural Revolution the party "put the capitalist intellectual
caps again on the intellectuals who already were declared a part of the
working class in early 1956."94 Deng Xiaoping pointed out in retrospect:
"To sum up the time before 1957, Comrade Mao Zedong's leadership was
correct, after the 1957 Anti-Rightist struggle errors just escalated." 1957
was when China turned "left" in the course of events. Looking back and
forward, it will be full of practical significance to remember the bitter experiences of 1957.

According to the verdict of the Twelfth National Convention of the
Chinese Communist Party held in 1982, the need in 1957 for such an Anti-
Rightist Campaign was greatly exaggerated and henceforth, the movement
was considered unduly expanded. However, the thing was done.

The verdict also noted nevertheless, that the Movement was both necessary and correct. The only thing wrong, it was said, was that the Movement was unduly expanded. Of course, citizen's rights damaged in 1957 were violated a hundred times more seriously in the Cultural Revolution years. "Nominally there is no official version[95] that the 1957 Anti-Rightist Movement was wrong, it still leaves four or five people considered rightists. The government admits the enlargement of the sphere, but that the Anti-Rightist movement was not wrong."[96]

Endnotes

1.   Chen Renbing unpublished biography
2.   Democratic League Secretary, Ke Shiji
3.   Chen Renbing unpublished biography
4.   Mao's exhortation: Let one hundred flowers bloom, let one hundred schools of thought contend" was first uttered at the Eleventh enlarged session of the Supreme State Conference in Beijing on February 27, 1957. However, it was not made public until June 19, 1957 after Mao revised it.
5.   The Selected Works of Mao Zedong, Volume V speech "Fight Back the Offensive of Bourgeois Rightists" July 9, 1957
6.   Volume Five was published posthumously in April 1977. The speech that mentions Chen as a culprit is found on pages 440-455 in the English version.
7.   On a February 27, 1982 visit to Chen, he told the author "Later you might hear from other sources, there were 22 rightists declared wrongly capped in June 1980 including Wang Zaoshi, Chang Laiqi. But, at the same time a decision was made that five members of Democratic Parties,the China Democratic League,and the September 3rd Party, were to be kept as bona fide rightists. That is they never were capped wrongly on national central level. Names of the five are:
1. Chu Anping London U. political science editor of "the Observer" editor and chief of the intellectuals newspaper, the Guang Ming Ri Bao.
2. Luo Longji, who took the exam for admittance to Qinghua Preparatory College in Jiangxi, and spent 8 years at Qinghua. He was American educated with a Ph.D. from Wisconsin. At the first China Democratic League organizational meeting 1941 March 19, Luo was elected to the executive committee. After 1949, he was a Vice-President of the League and Forestry Industry Minister. He died of high blood pressure in 1965.
3. Chen Renbing (1909-1990)
4. Zhang Bochun was German educated, graduating in 1941. At the first China Democratic League organizational meeting March 19, he was elected executive committee president. Zhang was Ministry of Transportation (other than railway) concerned with ocean vessels, boats etc.
5. Peng Wenyin Qinghua classmate of Luo Longji with a MA from Wisconsin in Political Science who died in 62 before the Cultural Revolution. Before 1949, he was professor of Shanghai Law College, but got no salary from anyone in 1957, however the political council gave special subsidy of 200 yuan. When he was demoted, they stopped subsidy and gave him only 30 yuan. He had five children,

one of them a Qinghua graduate. His wife died before he became a rightist; he never remarried.

8.   In the Chinese edition pages 448-450, in the English edition, pages 465-466

9.   Selected Works Volume V English version p. 449

10.   Mao's speech given to a Shanghai cadre conference. Selected Works of Mao Zedong Volume V. p. 457-472 "Beat Back The Attack Of The Bourgeois Rightists".

11.   In June 14, 1957 articles with headlines such as "Shanghai Committee of the Democratic League Exposes Internal Argument Against Chen Renbing and Finally Uncovers Wrong Thinking" The Beijing rightist mentioned is Zhang Bojun.

12.   In June 14, 1957 articles in various newspapers including the Wen Huibao and Jiefang Ribao (Liberation Daily)

13.   A written speech that he submitted to a conference convened by the Shanghai Committee of the Communist Party held in March 1957 was used to incriminate Chen.

14.   On June 9,1957 the second day after the end of the "open trap month", the *Liberation Daily* newspaper printed Chen's speech.

15.   This article appeared on the fifth day after Mao declared Chen a rightist. The June 14,1957, an editorial appeared in the *Liberation Daily* entitled "On the Clearing of Old Accounts." Chen was quoted in the June 15 *People's Daily*.

16.   In Chen Renbing's unpublished biography he is responding to the article in the (People's Daily)Renmin Ribao June 6, 1957.

17.   China's 100 Famous Big Rightists pp. 355-365

18.   China's 100 Famous Big Rightists pp. 355-365

19.   Shanghai Democratic League Central Committee member

20.   "Uncover Chen Renbing's Mistakes and Personal Ideology" July 14, 1957 Shanghai newspapers Wen Hui Bao and Jiefang Ribao

21.   In June 14, 1957 newspaper articles

22.   Another June 14 article from *Liberation Daily* and *Wen Hui Bao*, under the subheading, "Democratic League Central Committee Administrative Cadres Branch Meeting Expose"

23.   A *Liberation Daily* article of June 15, by Mr. Wu Zaohong entitled "I Do Not Agree With Chen Renbing's Ideas"

24.   "Chen Renbing's Premeditated Injury To The Party's Prestige"; "Chen Renbing's Sickly 'Fan the Flame' Article"; "Zhang Bojun Is A Two-Faced Person and Chen Renbing Vainly Hopes Rival Claim as an Equal"

25.   On July 6, the *Wen Hui Bao* newspaper exposed Chen's schemes at Shanghai Film Studio meetings held during November and December of 1956. The article, composed by Film Studio employees, states "we feel Chen's attitude is to make trouble and "fan the flames" of disorder; his speeches had a strong smell of gunpowder". They insist that all the subjects discussed at the forums, for example, film industry cadre leader's work style problems, leaders' opinions and ideas for movies, leaders attitudes toward using old movies, pay and conditions, management and system problems and divisions in film factory problems, Chen's motives were planned to embarrass the Party.

On the same page are several other anti-Chen articles, penned by members of Tonji University Democratic League and September 3rd Party members.

26.   A writer called Xu Dong, on June 24 in the Wen Hui Bao writes in a long article entitled "'Airing a View' of Rectification" that Chen Renbing's different views of rectification is a symbolic attack on the Party and socialism.

27.   The student, faculty, and staff meeting at East China Normal University was reported in the June 27 Liberation Daily that voiced critical opinions. "Chen Renbing already 'spread the fire' inside and outside dramatic circles. Three articles allege 'Party Secretary Reports On Different Classes' Reform Situation,' 'Welcome Comrades Outside the Party to Continue Criticizing' and 'Wake Up And Insist On Exposing Intellectual's Contradictions.' Other headlines read 'Exposure of Anti-Rightist Contradictions in the Cultural World is Not Strong Enough', 'Actors and Actresses Have to be More Sincere in Criticizing Rightist's Counterrevolutionary Activities' and 'The Shanghai Bar Association Members Very Strongly Support Struggling Against Rightists'.

Other pages in the same June 27 edition of the Liberation Daily are riddled with headlines, "Are We Really Going to Divide The Line With Chen Renbing, Or Continue An On-Again, Off-Again Relationship?", "The Film Industry Staff and Workers Emotions Are Roused to Action Calling the Party Branch to 'Clear This Account'"

28.   Chi 188

29.   Professor Tao Shaoyuan, alumnus of the University of Chicago.

30.   Interview with Tao Shaoyuan Shanghai Teachers University July 1992.

31.   Lu Yi, journalist who shared Chen's fate during the Anti-Rightist campaign.

32.   Ninety newspaper men 'had been ferreted out from press and radio operations all over China in the first stage of a struggle against Rightists in the journalistic field.' Lu emphasized that many intellectuals in academia got the same treatment.

33.   Lu was implicated in an article reported by the New York Times, "Red Chinese Purge Rightist Newsmen" reported from Hong Kong on July 26, that explains, "A purge of right-wing newspapermen has begun in Communist China, Xinhua News Agency reported."

34.   Lu Yi continued," Originally the Shanghai Mayor Zhu Rongji was Qinghua University rightist. The Shanghai woman vice-mayor Xie Lizhen also was a rightist. Now there is still one, Shanghai People's Representative, Chairman of the commission Ye Gongqi also was a rightist.

35.   Interview with Mr. Lu Yi

36.   Flip Flap was a college fraternity begun by Chinese students in the 1920's in the United States. Dr. Chen explained to the author that the name derived from a Broadway show. When Chen became a member, the alumnus in China were headed by Song Ziwen (T.V. Soong) and included Kong Xiangxi (H.H. Kung) and Wu Guodong as members. (infamous financiers under the Nationalist government) Chen Renbing retained an active membership upon returning home.

37.   *Zhan Wang*

38.   China's 100 Famous Big Rightists pp. 355-365

39.   Chen wrote in his unpublished biography "The list included well known director Wu Yunkang, actor Xiang Kun and actress Wu Yin. Miss Wu Yin had the distinction of being singled out as a "counter-revolutionary liner" in an article printed on page 448, Volume Five of the Selected Works of Mao Zedong. My humble name appears on the same page."

40. Xu Lei and Ye Shitao were the reporters who criticized Chen after the Wen Hui Bao (Shanghai newspaper) stirred up the "film bandwagon" controversy in November of 1956. Excerpts of their story:

As soon as the meeting began, Chen Renbing put on a sad face and pretended, in a warm atmosphere, to ask people to talk about the relationship between the masses and the Party. He lied to the people in the meeting saying that since the meeting was supported by the Shanghai Party Central Committee, everyone should feel free to talk or discuss. At the meeting some people said, "Today is the first time since liberation to have a "Democracy Day", some others said that in the Shanghai Film Factory they have maintained "nepotism," still others said the leaders of the Shanghai Film Factory were acting like "emperors" and the Party member are "enemy agents planted within our own ranks," criticizing the leaders makes you "go against your superiors".

In the meantime, Chen Renbing feigned surprise and interrupted to say, " When I hear " Democracy Day," "Nepotism ", " Go Against your Superiors," this kind of talk, it's very hard to take. I not going to blame those people for saying these kind of things, I find it strange why the Shanghai Film Factory still has this kind of opinion towards this kind of thing. The whole Shanghai film industry fire was just beginning, obsessed with ambition, Chen Renbing pushed himself to plot the movement, he wanted to burn down the film industry and burn down the Communist Party.

A famous film director was sick in the hospital, Chen Renbing made a special visit to him. At bedside, Chen Renbing respectfully and kindly talked. Then he changed the subject to the Zhongqing Cultural Movement during the War of Resistance Against Japan, and sadly remarked," Those were some ne'er do well friends, they have already become party members." But, look at that, you are a person of such progressive ideas and you are among the ones who have been forced out." You are no worse than those people, who else has the courage to play the communists party line? A lot of people they hired hid. You are the only one who stood up to take the whole responsibility. Look at you now......?" When the director heard this he said, "I blame myself for not trying hard enough." His heart had a fire, and he couldn't sleep all night. The feeling not to be satisfied toward the Party developed into sort of a hatred.

41. Delivered at the summer session of the Shanghai Assembly of People's Representatives

42. Chen considered that, "As a matter of fact, the political line of Deng Xiao Ping, in it's high estimation of China's intellectuals, I'm afraid, has the same starting point."

43. The full text of several accounts is as follows: Headline: "Security Scheme" and "Old Accounts: A long deep sigh and settling accounts, fanning the flame and a fanciful person's diversion"

Chen Renbing, was appointed as a member of the central committee of the China Democratic League in 1957. He was the vice-chairman of the Shanghai branch.

In 1957, Chen Renbing became famous for "settling old accounts," something which Chen Renbing himself did not anticipate. Of course, he really never expected that shortly after his "settling old accounts" infamy, that the name of Chen Renbing would be added to the list of "figures of public disgrace." Under Chen Renbing's name was written a ragged verse:

Trouble maker ignites hoping to cause calamity
A political hooligan's mark
Stale old accounts are outstanding bills due
Simultaneous settlement ought to be for both (Wen Hui Bao 1957.8.7)
On the contrary, before Chen Renbing had a chance to settle old accounts he himself became a debtor.
But, when Chen Renbing himself realized he became "a debtor," he perhaps already felt regret. But, everything was too late. A little while earlier, at a Shanghai committee member propaganda meeting, Chen Renbing presented his own views vehemently. That day he was very agitated. From April 27, when the Central Committee of the Chinese Communist Party indicated the rectification (movement for adjusting incorrect work styles), he was itching to have a go at it. Not long afterwards, when the United Front Committee again invited the China Democratic League faction to a discussion meeting, calling for uninhibited suggestions for Party and government, he was more excited.
"I hope the Party in this rectification is able to eliminate the trouble of crying bitter tears and heaving deep sighs of relief" (Ren Min Ri Bao 1957.6.15
What about the bill? Who's bill do we figure? What's the purpose? Repudiating a Debt?
In June 1957, less than 1 month after Chen Renbing's impassioned speech, some initiated a figuring of "Accounts" toward Chen Renbing. On the 14th, the Liberation Daily published an article entitled "On Settling Old Accounts" pointing out in all seriousness: Chen Renbing still has not openly written all his outstanding bills, but what account is he calculating, what is his purpose in settling accounts?
On the 16th, a writer called Ren Hui, also, in the People's Daily wrote: Chen Renbing and other rightists just want to settle new accounts, while seeming not to call up their own old accounts, I am inclined to be suspicious that he is going back on his word. Because, the accounts of Rightists, added all together, are not fully favored.
Again after 2 or 3 days, Deng Chuming, at an enlarged central committee meeting of the China Democratic League, also spoke about Chen Renbing's problem with settling accounts. 'He wants to settle new accounts, he wants to settle post-liberation Communist Party accounts, he wants to put forward several Communist Party members dispositions. It is acceptable to settle new accounts, there is no fear of settling them, I see that it is just the old accounts better not be settled, also they cannot be settled clearly. We intellectuals carried over from the old society, ought to take our conscience out and speak heart to heart. Except for a few people, in the old society what did we old-timers contribute, any sort of good things, or any sort of dirty deals.(Renmin Ribao 1957.6.19)
On the night of the 12th, the Shanghai branch of the China Democratic League continued its discussion meeting. Chen Renbing attended the session. During the meeting, the members launched face to face criticism towards Chen Renbing.
"Perhaps, my speech at the propaganda meeting 1 month ago has a contradiction compared with the Party's guiding principle and steps. Because, at that time, I didn't hear Comrade Ke Qingshi's statement, and I didn't understand the points of the rectification instruction," Chen Renbing explained." I had an idea to inflict punishment for misconduct, and I didn't understand the point of instruction."
"Chen Renbing, 2 days ago at the Cadres meeting you still said, you were very worried about this Party rectification, because rectification has to have some achieve-

ment, what if the task isn't carried out?" Wu Nan said. Professor Su Buqin, famous mathematician also attended the meeting and made accusations against Chen Renbing (Wen Hui Bao 1957.6.14)

This meeting was very animated. At 11:00 P.M., there were still many people who wanted to speak, but the chairman

ended the session and allowed that the meeting would continue at a later date.

It was reported that no sooner had Chen Renbing finished his self-criticism than Zhou Yutong said, "Your self-criticism is dishonest. You still juggle various political means, this cannot be forgiven." "Newspapers expose much more than you yourself say, you ought to more honestly, frankly and remorsefully confess" (Wen Hui Bao 1957.6.14).

Tian Rukan said, "Chen Renbing already said he would come to each meeting if his ideological thinking was to be criticized; and at worst, he just made some self-criticism In the least, as a professor, he can't escape making self-criticism. Today his demeanor is just like this. Truthfully, we won't tolerate his bullying.

Professor Qiu Riqing went on to say, "When you all were in Beijing and Shanghai, how were things discussed with, Luo Longji, Zhang Bojun? What sort of thing is it when you were singing the same tune? Chen Renbing is an unscrupulous person who cares not for the interests of the people but for advancing his own position, he's adept at trickery. Chen Renbing shouldn't make fools of others, he ought to be honest and frank", said History department chair Tan Qixiang.

44.   Quoted in China's One hundred famous big rightists, p. 355365 Ren Min Ri Bao (People's Daily) 1957.6.15

45.   China's One hundred famous big rightists quote of Wen Hui Bao article 1957.6.14

46.   Chen Renbing unpublished biography

47.   China's One hundred famous big rightists quote of Wen Hui Bao article 1957.6.14

48.   The People's Daily July 14, 1957 editorial said I was the first person in south China to be branded a "rightist". The article,"On Clearing of Old Accounts" was full of slander, putting words in my mouth which I have never said either in my June 9 article nor anywhere else. The editorial alleged that China's "rightists" lamented the liberation of China and took achievements of the People's government as some old accounts which needed to be settled.

49.   Chen Renbing (unpublished) biography

50.   Chen Renbing (unpublished) biography

51.   Chen Renbing (unpublished) biography

52.   "What sort of Other Road is Chen Renbing Taking?" on June 26, 1957 was written by Wu Song, a pseudonym revealed in the *History of Zhang Chunqiao*. Articles were published in the *Liberation Daily* on June 14, 1957 and another editorial attack on Chen in the Liberation Daily on June 27, 1957.

53.   Five short articles are within the feature's boundaries on July 2, including two against Dr. Chen Renbing entitled, "Chen Renbing and Lan Yishi Are of The Same Family", by Chen Binggui and "Jackals From The Same Lair" by Shi Du. Again, on July 5, in "ALL THE RIGHTIST' FACES" feature, is an article entitled, "This Is How Chen Renbing Lured Me to Join the China Democratic League" by Dong Ailin, a famous singer. Miss Dong reports:

After the newspaper uncovered Chen Renbing's ugly face, it made me understand how Rightist Chen Renbing uses different ploys to recruit members...(to) support his position as an anti-party political base...his goal is to knock down socialism.

I was also approached by Chen to become a bird of the same feather...at the beginning of this year Zhou Zhenlan, already mentioned to me his hope that I could join the league. I didn't accept his suggestion. Not longer afterwards, the Democratic League noticed and twice again invited me to a discussion meeting. I really didn't want to join, therefore I never went once.

In March, Chen Renbing, through Zhou Zhenlan, invited me to dinner. At the time I thought it was to influence me to join the League, therefore I didn't want to accept. I happened to run into him (Chen) at a small club meeting. We exchanged greetings. After a week Chen again went through Zhou Zhenlan to invite me to have dinner at the Cultural Club. At that time I was undecided. So Zhou Zhenlan said, 'Twice you refused his invitation, it doesn't matter if you join the Democratic League, he just wants to invite you to dinner. If you refuse again, it wouldn't be very nice'. At the same time I thought to myself, 'To ask someone to eat, and then, not to say, that along with eating (together), I also want you to join league. A person (Chen) kind of loses face. So, I went together with Zhou Zhenlan.

During dinner, Chen Renbing was talking about his love for music, representing himself as an aficionado. Eventually we talked about the party. He said, 'If you open the newspaper's theater advertisement section, you will see that many opera stars are Democratic League Members, In the local theater, we have Ding Shier. In the music world there aren't as many. Especially in music, members who are singers are very few, therefore we encourage you singers to join us'. At the time I heard it I was shocked. What kind of organization is it when you have to point out if members are famous people or not, just name dropping. It caused me to be very strongly against it. As a result I had no interest in joining.

After about another week, Chen Renbing came to my home. He again encouraged me to join. At the time I wanted to express that I still wasn't prepared to join the party. Chen Renbing said, 'I hope this is not your final decision, I still ask you to please reconsider'. The strangest thing is, at the same time, his friend Mr. Mou talked to me and said, 'Mr. Chen Renbing is not very likely to go to people's home and talk to them'. After he said that to me, it seemed like I should feel like I'm very honored to have him recruit me. Chen Renbing must feel like I'm on equal footing." I feel I have must write about this thing, to make people understand what methods Chen Renbing uses to recruit the members for the League. It certainly isn't from a warm desire to elevate political and ideological education. It's not a good way to start things up, by using eating dinner and visiting you and hanging around, planning to recruit his political base and foundation. Next to Miss Dong's expose, is another article, critical of Dr. Chen for his "Stubborn Way to Destroy College Organization's Improving Conditions" written by Zhou Xiaoping. Hua Dong Normal University is still "Strongly Criticizing Theater Propaganda" in an article written by Bai Ge.

54.   This caricature appears in the July 7, 1957 *Wen Hui Bao* under an article entitled, "The Staff of Shanghai Film Studio Rally to Reprove Chen Renbing's Opinion"

55.   "Under the Microscope-The Anti-Party Action of Chen Renbing, penned by a 'Wen Hui Bao Editor'

56.   In the New York Times July 2, 1957 special from Hong Kong

57.   Xinhua News Agency

58.   NY Times July 6, 1957 5:3

59.   NY Times July 6, 1957 5:3

60.   Selected Works of Mao Zedong Vol.5 Foreign Language Press Beijing, 1977 English edition pp. 448-450

61.   Selected p. 448

62.   NY Times July 2, 1957 4:8

63.   NY Times July 2, 1957 4:8

64.   This was originally printed in the newspaper popular among intellectuals, the Guangming Ribao on July 13, 1957.

65.   Chen Renbing unpublished biography

66.   The remaining text of the article which is surprisingly similar to the Dong Ailin article, reads: 'Chen Renbing often said: " So long as we can win over several public figures in some work units we will control the situation. " In order to capture the famous figures, by hook or by crook, pay somebody a visit, invite someone to dinner, send a car or other despicable methods, going so far as to allow them not to take an oath, not to write a resume, not participate in meetings as bait to induce them to join. Famous Shanghai singer, Huang Ai Lin, was a target. Chen Renbing, who first used relationships with others, invited her to attend the discussion meeting, and invited her for dinner several times. Huang Ai Lin refused. At last, Huang had no way out, and managed with difficulty to agree once with his request. At the dinner party, he proclaimed how much he loved music, following up by proclaiming to Huang, Ailin, flaunting that in the field of Shangai Opera we have Ding Shier on our side, in Shaoxing opera we have Qi Yaxian, in Beijing opera we have etc...it's just that in music circles, League people are too few, especially among singers there are even fewer, therefore I hope you famous singers are also able to participate..." This kind of talk gave rise to Huang Ai Lin's intense disgust, immediately she refused to join the League, but Chen Renbing did not drop the matter. One week later, he went running to Huang Ai Lin's home to persuade her to join the League. However, after Huang Ai Lin flatly refused, Chen Renbing still brazen-faced said: "I still hope this is not your last decision, I still ask you to think about it."
At the time of uncovering Chen Renbing's guilt a letter Teng Baiye, Shanghai Traditional Chinese Painting Society member, gave Chen Ren Bing was revealed. In the letter Teng Baiye said: Elder Brother Ren Bing: 'If there is unexpected praise, or unattainable demands for perfection, remain unperturbed. You never surrender you ideals to hatchet men. If your opinion on public affairs is from the bottom of your heart then you have to believe in yourself, don't be afraid of anything, advocate and persevere to the end, you no longer need to do self-criticism.
Teng Baiye belonged in the category of "Stubborn Rightists", Chen Renbing didn't accept his advice, he also didn't dare accept it. Not long after, he gave a self-criticism again, thoroughly unmasking himself.(Wen Hui Bao 1957.9.6)

67.   On July 18, a *People's Daily*

68.   China's One Hundred Famous Big Rightists, pp. 355-365

69.   Chen implicated others saying, "Peng, Sun and I were the nucleus, along with Han and others were the backbone, Shen Zhiyuan cooperated with us to form an anti-party clique."

70.   Wen Hui Bao 1957.9.6

71.   Leaders of the minor parties that the Communists have permitted to hold office...are under heavy pressure for having attacked the Government during the

last few weeks. Dr. Luo Longji, Zhang Bochun and Zhang Naiqi are the main targets of the pressure. News broadcasts from Beijing...charged that Zhang Bojun and Dr. Luo had a plan to organize a party of "several million intellectuals to struggle for leadership in China (and)...implied that Mr. Zhang and Dr. Luo sought to take power from the Communist Party.

72.   NY Times July 5, 1957 4:6

73.   NY Times July 5, 1957 4:6

74.   In a July 15, 1957 Hong Kong article, reported in the NY Times on July 16,

75.   Chi 189

76.   Chi 188

77.   Chi 188,189

78.   A rightist cap awaited such persons. To be branded a rightist was no light matter. Treatment (or punishment) was meted out at the pleasure of leftist colleagues. A "rightist" might be sent to labor camp in remote provinces like Xinjiang or Qing Hai or Heilongjiang. Or, they might be sent to places of labor nearby.

Suggestions for novel improvements, for example, that the Party pay more attention to experts and scholars in factories and colleges, was often thought to belittle the Party's leadership and may be taken as Anti-Party sentiment.

79.   Among the six were Dr. Fei Xiaotong, Dr. Chien Weichang and Dr. Ceng Chaolung.

80.   Chen Renbing said, "As far as children were concerned, my friend Dr. Wang Zaoshi seemed to be luckier. Dr. Wang Zaoshi, my Fudan colleague, was similarly punished. Yet, Dr. Wang and I belonged to a better class He had four, two sons, two daughters. His "crime" was suggesting that the authorities take council from wise advisors, just as the old Tang dynasty emperor listened to the advice of Viceroy Wei Chen.

Dr. Wang's wife died most inopportunely, on the eve of his being branded. His eldest daughter graduated from Ginling College and was a quiet pianist who lived a life of melancholy. When her father was capped "rightist", she committed suicide. His second daughter, Wang Hai Yong, Fudan University physics senior, was recalcitrant over her father's ill luck and protested his innocence, maintaining he was not anti-Party or anti-socialist. For her pains, she was also branded.

Wang's two sons were emotionally unbalanced to begin with. When the papers splashed Dr. Wang's "guilts," their minds became further unhinged and they were sent to the largest mental hospital in Shanghai, cases of schizophrenia. The boys died a few years later in the hospital. Later on, his remaining daughter died of cancer. So closed the Wang chapter, father and daughter "rightist" team."

81.   Chen Renbing (unpublished) biography

82.   Chen Renbing (unpublished) biography

83.   Across the highway from the mental hospital where one of his colleagues, Dr. Wang Zaoshi's's two sons were kept inmates.

84.   Chen continues," Among us were Dr. Wang Zaoshi, Mr. Sheng Chihyuan, famous reporters Lu Yi and Hsu Chucheng, as well as some businessmen, textile mill and factory heads and other so-called people with some "face," that is members of the local Political Consultative Council or People's Representatives.

85.   Some "rightists" over age 60, were allowed to stay in the city and attend study sessions there. They included men like the great painter Mr. Liu Haishou and the well-known translator of books like John Christopher, Mr. Fu Luei.

86.   Interview with Mr. Liu Yi 2:00 P.M. Thursday July 9, 1992 at his home on Wu Kang Road in Shanghai
87.   Chen Renbing (unpublished) biography
88.   Including, Wang Zaoshi and Lu Yi.
89.   Also mentioned by name were Fang Shulun, Huang Huo, Wu Yonggan, Li Binghuan, Fang Zifan, Wang Zhong, Lin Tongji, Wang Ruowang, and Zhang Jinting.
90.   Ministry of Defense Vice Minister Wang Zhezhong made the announcement.
91.   Chen Renbing (unpublished) biography
92.   Ye Yonglie 1993/5 *Heavy Hearted 1957* Publishing Company *The Misery of 1957* Bai Hua Ji Volume 81 is *Heavy Hearted 1957*'s continuation.
93.   Li Weihan was a senior member of the Communist Party. He's from Changsha, Hunan Province and was born in 1896 as Li Hesheng, with the nickname Luo Mai. Early in 1918, he and Mao Zedong, Cai Hesen organized the New People's Association in Changhsha. In 1922, when he joined the Communist Party, he was introduced by Mao and Cai. He was on the Political Bureau of the Fourth and Fifth Central Committee of the Party respectively. In 1927, he was the main organizer and chairman of the "8.7 Meeting" together with Qu Qiubai and Su Zhaozheng organized a temporary central committee. Afterwards, he had the posts of central organizing committee head of party's secretary of Shanxi and Gansu Provinces, and Yenan central party school principal. In 1948, he became the head of the United Front Committee and held the position until 1964. He held that job longer than anyone did. In 1979, he came back to the government and still was an advisor to the United Front Committee. You can say he was the "United Front Senior Statesman."
94.   The text continues: In his *Recollections and Considerations*, Li Weihan spoke sincerely and honestly about 1957:
"Towards the Central Committee and Mao Zedong's position concerning class struggle, I guess that the anti-rightist struggle course and organization, in my mind, had no bad feeling (suspicions) one way or another. I'm afraid I can't follow the situation, guiding my thought toward the "left." Because of this, I firmly put into effect the Party's instructions among the Democratic League's industrial and business circles, and outside party people.
Although Li Weihan feared "falling behind the whole situation" and "implemented firmly" several "left" policies, he couldn't avoid being regarded as a "revisionist," "capitulationist" and being criticized in October 1962, when the Tenth Plenary Session of the Party Central Committee put forth the slogan "Never Forget Class Struggle." The United Front Committee held meetings at the ministerial level to criticize Li Weihan more than 40 times in six months.
In 1963, Li Weihan wrote "Political Policy Errors" in which he referred to : "Eliminating the Capitalist Class" in several decades. This is Li's "deepened understanding" after he already was criticized more than forty times. The report was sent to Chairman Mao. Mao added another line, this is to just to say, in China carrying out "class struggle," will last for as long as "one hundred years".
Li Weihan still can't follow the situation. In 1964, again he was criticized by the United Front. The same year in December, he was removed from the post as head of the United Front.

Successively, a storm of "Class Struggle" which was, according to Chen Renbing, "ten times, a hundred times" fiercer than the Anti-Rightist Struggle swept across China. A 10-year long catastrophe befell. Li Weihan was thrown into prison and was sent to Xian Ning, Hubei Province, for more than 8 years during which he got tubercular peritonitis and experienced the ruthless "Class Struggle" himself.

Having suffered great disaster and difficulties, Li Wenhan became sober and clear-headed. On reflection and pondering, this 80-year old man began to write the 1,000,000 character book, *Recollections and Considerations.*

He reviewed his opinions and speeches in 1957, with all sorts of emotions:

"The articles and speeches I put forth during that time showed a lack of overall and historical analysis. Toward democratic parties which have cooperated with our party for a long time and have been declared the class-alliance, I simply asserted that "In the past and now they all were capitalist political practices."

95.   According to Dr. Tan Jiazhen, a full member of the United States Academy of Science since 1985 and current chairman of the Shanghai China Democratic League

96.   Interview with Tan Jiazhen July 4, 1992 Shanghai

11. 1948 Marcus and Mary Chen in the United States.

12. 1951 *Marcus and Mary Chen in Beijing.*

13. *1952 Mary, Renbing, and Marcus Chen.*

14. *1956 Chen Renbing giving speech while vice-chairman of the Shanghai Democratic League. Portrait of Mao Zedong looms in the background.*

15. 1972 Chen Renbing in Shanghai.

16. 1982 Chen Renbing during an interview session in his Shanghai apartment.

17. 1984, January 19. Chen Renbing, wife Yuin Hwei Chen and son Chen Jiaxin taken on their twentieth wedding anniversary.

18. Caricature of Chen Renbing with "money" written on his heart, holding a "flame" and dancing on a western music record. The caricature appeared on 7 July 1957 in the Wen Hui Bao newspaper in Shanghai. The accompanying article is entitled "Chen Renbing Fanning the Flame of Anti-Party Sentiment."

右派分子在"搽粉"了。

·顧炳鑫作

19. *Caricature of Chen Renbing which appeared in the Liberation Daily newspaper on 27 June 1957 with the caption "A Rightist putting on his 'makeup'."*

章罗集团驻沪"主将"槍法已乱
陈仁炳吞吞吐吐交代
人們要他老老实实徹底交代关鍵性問題

陳 仁 炳

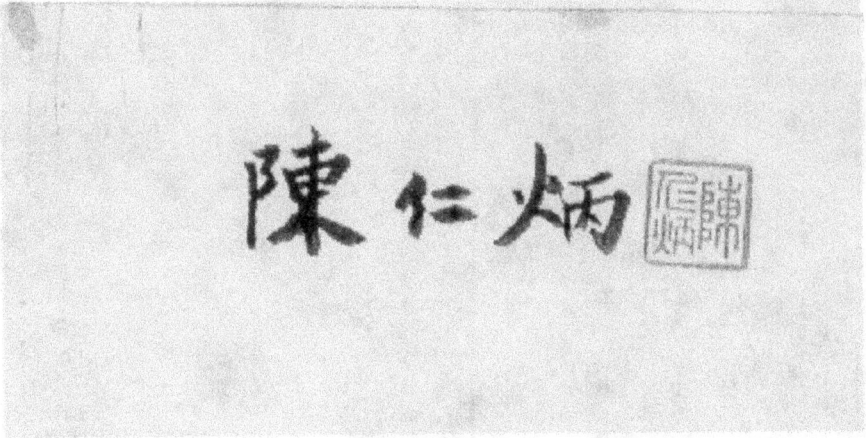

21. Chen Renbing's own calligraphy and personal seal.

22. *Obituary notices from Fudan University and Shanghai newspapers.*

Chapter V: The Aftermath

LEADERSHIP OF TERROR

The so-called Great Proletarian Cultural Revolution lasted 10 chaotic years from 1966 to 1976. The movement was spearheaded by Mao Zedong and ultra-left Chinese leaders Jiang Qing,[1] Zhang Chunqiao,[2] Yao Wenyuan and Wang Hongwen who came to be known as the "Gang of Four." For intellectuals, the dominant characteristic of the Cultural Revolution was rewarding those who were "red", or blindly loyal to the mixture of Marxist-Leninist-Mao Zedong Thought, and punishing those who were "expert," espoused capitalism or, who relied on book learning. The Gang of Four had their own agenda. They led communist cadres toward determining the virtuous from the criminal and were responsible for enlarging the Cultural Revolution to include intellectuals.[3]

Regular schools were suspended while the government instituted attacks on all "representatives of the bourgeoisie" who had infiltrated the Party, government, army and cultural world. Citizen's rights were endlessly violated, rendering useless precepts of constitutional law. Remote areas[4] of the country did not escape the wild outings by rebellious groups who wantonly destroyed places like ancestral temples and libraries. Terrorized people made false confessions and turned in family and friends in the name of revolution.

Urban students were sent to the countryside to "learn from the peasants." High school and college age party members, known as "Red Guards," were led by fanatical Communist cadres to invade people's homes, and cart off anything deemed a "bourgeois" influence.

Red guards roamed free of charge on trains, steamships, buses and streetcars all over China's vast provinces on so-called "inter-provincial grand liaison tours." No one dared ask for fares and risk being charged a counter-revolutionary. While Fudan University in Shanghai was overflowing with students from Beijing, Guangzhou, Xian and Fuzhou, Shanghai students were likely to be visiting Tianjin, Harbin, Hankou and Zhongqing.

During the Cultural Revolution targeted intellectuals were publicly ridiculed as "oxen demons and serpent spirits". They lost all status and rights for 10 years, had their homes ransacked and sometimes confiscated by Red Guards and were physically abused, sometimes tortured to death. It seemed to many that they stood at the crossroads of extinction. Suicides were commonplace.

At the beginning of the movement, large character posters attacked old thoughts, old cultures, old customs and old habits. General anarchy was the nemeses of culture and negation of the Chinese Revolution. Law and order, sanity and common sense were lost.[5] Chen Renbing's friend explained:

> Mao Zedong made people fight and kill each other in a way that has been done only in Chinese history. It was the most notable thing he had ever done. During the Cultural Revolution, there was a mania beyond reason. It is impossible to explain this tragedy of Chinese intellectuals.[6]

Mao's supporters argued his theory of the spiral process of history, the "unification of theory and practice' foreshadowed both the Cultural Revolution and educational revolution.[7] Education veered toward technology. The humanities were deliberately neglected unless they were linked with political ideological education. Ideologues declared the educational revolution was a struggle between two classes. The two roads were Chairman Mao's proletarian educational line and the counterrevolutionary revisionist educational line. Respective to the horror of the Cultural Revolution, the Educational Reform of 1952 and Anti-Rightist purge of 1957 were mild. A former rightist friend of Chen Renbing spoke of Mao's power and his personal experience:

> When the chairman criticized, those on the sidelines went along with him. We only had the right to go along with him in accompanying the person being criticized because we were rightists and were already beaten down. We already were dead tigers, without power. Capitalism, socialism, it didn't matter to us."[8]

Living through the Cultural Revolution, meant a fight for survival. People's attitude was, 'I am protecting myself from you. You are protecting yourself from me. You 'struggle' me and I 'struggle' you.' Individuals needed to defend themselves when talking to others, creating a chasm impossible to bridge. People realized they were unable to treat each other sincerely. Interpersonal relationships were bad, and they still have not completely recovered to normal. It will not happen so fast. To intellectuals, this process had it's beginnings from the influence of the 1950 Thought Reform.[9]

During the Cultural Revolution, the goal of the government seemed to be to expunge any fragments of outside influence and deify the communist party. Physical evidence of this phenomenon are the millions of porcelain, plastic and medal "Mao Buttons" manufactured by work units nationwide that each citizen wore every day. Everyone sported their own collection and changed their buttons often.[10]

Formal education was disdained because of the danger that people might think for themselves and discover the party was not acting in their best interests. Intellectuals were subjugated to manual labor to reverse roles with peasants. Workers and peasants were considered the only worthwhile citizens because they engaged in the means of production and tangibly contributed to nation building. Intellectuals may have known theory, but in the skewed logic of the day, they were too far removed from practice to be of any value. The leadership sanctioned their humiliation and ruined careers because their inability to successfully perform manual labor would illustrate their worthlessness.

Mao had a famous saying, "The more intellectuals you have, the more counter-revolutionaries you have." Intellectuals interviewed for this work were asked to comment on Mao's words. One responded, "Mao decided students needed no formal education, and people were discouraged from reading a wide variety of books. If Mao said, 'Go east,'" they went east. This is meaningless. He had no world vision, no broad outlook. Skilled surgeons were kept away from the operating tables, mathematics professors were ordered to perform manual labor, a Chinese literature expert was ordered to sweep the streets for 8 years, and later he and his family were dispatched to take care of oxen in a southern village.[11]

Being sent to the hinterlands was common punishment for "enemies of the people" and many had no recourse to ever return to their original homes. The Cultural Revolution lasted so long and affected every possible segment of Chinese people's lives. It's effects are hard to measure, much less fathom. The rightists were really afflicted, particularly those like Professor Chen Renbing who were patriotic, devoted and contributed to education.[12]

TEN YEARS OF CHAOS

Chen's Odessy During the Cultural Revolution

Chen Renbing's personal storm began anew in July 1965 when he was demoted from the teaching staff of Fudan University to the position of laborer when he "got trapped again when one day there was a big character poster at the Fudan University gate signed by the president saying

that since being named a Rightist I had failed to reform myself thoroughly."[13]

The poster proclaimed Chen's moral quality made him unfit for teaching and as a result his position in the history department was canceled.
Chen recalled:

> While a mass meeting in the History Department was convened, I was
> called to another room. Two officials told me I was deemed unsuitable
> as a teacher. I wrote so many confessions because they accused me of
> giving private dancing parties and later named four different friends
> who borrowed my place in 1962, maybe seven or eight times. Since I
> had a living room of 40 square meters, why not use the room for danc-
> ing? Nobody said they shouldn't.
>
> They called the offense giving "black-out parties" when we had green
> and red lights. The officials called me terrible things, things made up,
> and said I was unfit for college teaching. 'We are planning what to do
> with you.
>
> You have two choices, either we dismiss you as a teacher and you do
> labor reform in the university, or, we'll give you over to the police'.
>
> Before 10:00 A.M. one Saturday morning in April, speeches were given
> and they decided to send me to some place in our university to do
> labor. At the end of the meeting, the department took me to the per-
> sonnel department. Then personnel took me to the department of gen-
> eral affairs, and called the head of the carpentry shop saying, 'We hand
> Chen over to you, from now on he's under your charge'. Thus I report-
> ed to the workshop at 2:00 P.M. that day and worked there until I
> retired on May 29, 1974. This is how I became a worker.
>
> The clerk in the personnel department with a long face asked me what
> I was supposed to get. They fixed my salary as a new member, a col-
> lege graduate at Y60.00 a month. After 1 week I was called to person-
> nel. They said: 'We've reconsidered your pay and raised it to Y82.50 a
> month'. When I was forced to retire, I got a retirement fee at Y57.75
> between 1974-1980. They only gave me Y30.00 a month during the
> Cultural Revolution. It was not until November 1981 that I received
> my original pre-rightist salary of Y218."[14]

At the beginning of the Cultural Revolution, Professor Chen was held in
Number Four dormitory at Fudan University, separated and supervised. He
wasn't allowed to associate with anybody. No legal proceedings were followed and therefore his detention was illegal.

Chen spent those years, when not "segregated", making bricks, fixing
stoves, carting wood shavings. However, working electric and mechanical
saws was his main duty. Sometimes, he was ordered to climb on roof tops
to fix tin chimneys, or, to clean gutters. For years, the Red Guards affiliated

with Fudan University cut his salary to only Y30.00 a month. The Chen family lived on bread and rice for months on end, with no meat. For at least 6 years Chen subsisted on noodle soup for breakfast, a wheat cake for lunch and, at Y4¢ a bowl, rice with vegetable soup for supper.

In as much as Fudan had no provisions for serving thousands and thousands of meals to hoards of roaming Red Guards, they could not let the Grand Liaison Scholars go hungry. In winter, cabbage was cheap and in summer, white gourds were all Fudan could afford. After days of being fed on gourd soup and rice, Chen recalls that "our guests pasted huge posters on campus proclaiming "What, More White Gourds? No More White Gourds For Us, Please!"[15]

During the Cultural Revolution at Fudan University, it was chaotic and confused. At that time, Fudan separated into two revolutionary factions. School rebels, Chao Fan Pai, were divided and civil war between them went on day and night, to the destruction of the class rooms and library. Thousands of windows were smashed and members of both sides were wounded. Chen Renbing was careful to draw back and mind his own labor because he was an "oxen devil and serpent spirit."

China stood paralyzed economically as dog fights between cliques of "revolutionary" camps nationwide created cultural stagnation and waste. Individuals rounded up in the 1957 Anti-Rightist Campaign were again singled out in vast numbers from 1966-1976. Many "rightists" did not survive the stern trials and when the Cultural Revolution began, many were still exiled in Chinese Turkistan, Qinghai Province or the freezing northeast, serving out their "reform through labor." The burden of these 10 years added more bitterness to their cups.

Chen was compelled to retire in 1974 at age 65 with only 70% of his manual laborer's salary. Chen was "moved" by Red Guardsmen to a slum where, as a retired worker, he lived with his wife and son for 2 years. Chen recalled that most of their neighbors were wonderful and they treated the involuntary newcomers with friendship. All of Chen's neighbors knew the head rebel at Fudan University confiscated his apartment. Ironically, Chen's friend explained, "The very party secretary who vilified Chen got into trouble during the Cultural Revolution. The Red Guards dug out his pre-revolution past revealing he had gambled his wife away! It was then his turn to be displayed on the stage with 100 people shouting at him."[16]

Chen said that most of his neighbors were textile workers, chemical product factory workers or steel workers. At first, Chen explained, in spite of the disruption created by the Cultural Revolution, life seemed to go on as usual for the working people. But on second thought, Chen admitted it was not so because in some of the largest steel factories, there emerged two camps of worker rebels, each engaged in life and death fights with the opposite camp.

Chen and his wife worried about fulfilling duties of a neighborhood project when the quiet kindness of a neighbor demonstrated more respect for him and his family than the government was willing to offer him as an intellectual:

> Once, for the purpose of making bricks for some kind of public works project, each house and family was ordered to contribute about 100 kilograms of mud clay. My wife and I did not know what to do, because we did not have the necessary spades or rattan baskets. On the third morning, we found a big pile of mud clay by our door, weighing no less than the requirement.
>
> Later, we learned that this was the kind act of a woman worker living across the lane from us. Her occupation was carting commodities and she used her pushcart to transport enough mud clay, quietly unloading it in front of our home.[17]

What was life like for intellectuals during the Cultural Revolution? Few people of Chen's class escaped the fate of having personal possessions looted and being forced to give up their homes. There was no peace in daily life, not even short breathers, for most teachers, professors, authors, educators, doctors, actors, artists, musicians, Church leaders or former business people. A considerable number of individuals were forced to accept large cuts in income and the more unfortunate were banished to the hinterlands or the vast northeast plains. The universal lament is that in the struggling, the accuser became the accused, and, many died.

DENOUEMENT

Chen Renbing's 90-year old mother could not stand the shock of his troubles and moved to his sister, Martha's apartment in another part of Shanghai. "Poor mother did not learn of Joel's cruel death until 5 years later. The Gang of Four forbade victim's families from knowing their fates. So, mother and I were ignorant of the bad news for several years. I think even Hitler would not have kept a victim's mother from being informed of her son's death. Mother died on March 31, not long after learning about Joel."[18]

When ruin seemed unavoidable, there appeared to be another side to the picture. Dissatisfaction was accumulating, revealing a limit to people's patience. For years all was not quiet in the Party and opposition fermented. People saw Zhou Enlai as helpless, yet he remained an image in people's minds as a symbol of sanity and moral resistance. A burgeoning consensus began to expose the indestructible will of the Chinese people. On April 5, 1976, during the Qing Ming season of memorial for the dead, thousands of wreaths dedicated to Premier Zhou and Madame Yang Kai Hui (Mao's first wife) were laid about Tian An Men Square. Chen writes,

> Jiang Qing, who managed to make everyone hate her, could not miss that the eulogies to her rival condemned her. Zhang Chunqiao could not fail to read that the people's love for Premier Zhou, vented pent up hate for him and his Gang. The Gang ordered all the offending laurels removed. However, loyal mourners persisted and the next night they sent steel-framed wreaths that could not be destroyed and kept vigilance over the new batch of flowers. Violence and manslaughter ensued, but the people won. This conflict served as a signal to the common folk to rise against Jiang Qing and all that she stood for. What was once invincible came crashing down. The Cultural Revolution was finally over.[19]

After the Cultural Revolution ended in 1976, many secrets of the Party were exposed. Intellectuals discovered that the government had demanded too much of them. In China today, intellectuals say there are two kinds of older intellectuals, those whose backbones were broken and those who were not. After the Cultural Revolution human relations did not fully recover. One intellectual explained, "You know in history people always share difficulties. During the war people were united because they shared a common opinion towards the war. Now it's different. Going through the Cultural Revolution, one had to use a different strategy to fight. Some relations have recovered because people tend to forget, but tension still exists because people were made to criticize each other."[20]

> The Cultural Revolution was bad and abnormal for China and it's people.[21] It is natural for one to speak out, to say what is right. For a long time, people clinging to that idea could not be tolerated in China. During the Cultural Revolution, Mao decided that students should break off their education, leave the classrooms to do labor and learn from the peasants.[22]

Intellectuals related that their attitude and view had gradually changed after the Cultural Revolution because of the growing commercialism in China. Some described modern times as every single eye staring at money while things that should be done are left undone. Some intellectuals sadly reported that since the end of the Cultural Revolution, many Party members have engaged in unfair businesses and thus become corrupt. People today read about the lives and histories of Mao's children as well as[23] other leaders and voice the same concerns about people not caring about culture and just going after money.[24]

> It is said that many people are becoming richer and richer. Yet, I personally am still suspicious of those who have become rich. The Communist Party got rid of all classes. But now they set up their own

class. All their people together with their children become the ruling class. This I can't understand.

Neither do many other intellectuals. Since the open door policy in China, our country had too much attention on economy and education, morality as well as culture have been given cold shoulders. This we can't understand. It is true that many people have become rich. To have money is not a bad thing. But those who should have money don't have money and those who shouldn't have become rich.[25]

Post-Cultural Revolution

After the Cultural Revolution, China passed through 2 years of hesitancy and then 4 more years adjusting from disturbance toward regularity. Intellectuals entered a new vista of material and cultural growth. In Chen Renbing's opinion, the secret to Deng Xiaoping's success in the few years since he took over the helm of a broken and exhausted nation was continuing the late Premier Zhou Enlai's great tradition of making friends with Chinese intellectuals. Deng's own political career had been in jeopardy during earlier political movements, and, having been abroad himself, he realized that in order for China to advance, conditions for intellectuals must improve and their contributions nurtured. Chen Renbing spoke for himself and other intellectuals of his generation when he said, "Chinese intellectuals love China dearly. They return friendship with sincerity, and, through the democratic parties, channel their patriotism and devotion to the people."[26]

Some 15 years after the end of the Cultural Revolution Chen Renbing's friend said, "One of the greatest tragedies of the Cultural Revolution is the deterioration of human relations because people still are too reluctant to trust anyone. Some relations have recovered because people tend to forget, but tension still exists because people were made to criticize other people. During the Cultural Revolution, everyone was forced to expose their deepest thoughts and nothing could be hidden. Everybody knew everybody else and what you had done. So, it was a test of your character.[27]

Although intellectuals may have been rectified in some year, or returned to a professional position, the feeling from their interviews is that they feel awkward to meet some people and to avoid painful memories. The situation for intellectuals remained precarious even after the close of the Cultural Revolution. The Chinese Public Security Bureau, had secret files in the police department for everyone who was a returned student from the United States or Europe. Chen's friend explained how all the intellectuals that came back from abroad were shadowed. "During the Cultural

Revolution they dug up the files from the police department. Later on after the fall of the Gang of Four, these files were made public. Documents were returned to the owner. I didn't receive back all the documents I lost, they gave me a part of it, what I had written."[28] Ruan Ming, a Deng Xiaoping insider who was Deputy Director of the Theoretical Research Department until 1983 described the situation in the spring of 1980 when the central propaganda department held a forum to discuss the problem of the intellectuals:

> Military dogmatists got together with like-minded allies in the Party to launch an attack on the wave of reformers that were now approaching the cities. Their slogan was 'Promote proletarian ideology and eliminate bourgeois ideas.' Hu Yaobang had requested I write an article to be entitled "Policy Toward Intellectuals", that he wanted to have published in the People's Daily under the byline "special commentator." But in the face of opposition the People's Daily refused and there began a call "the time has come to launch and attack on "liberalism." The object of this debate escaped me, and I know very little about the issue of intellectuals. The real issue now is to struggle against liberal ideas and policies. The problem now is to launch and attack on liberalism. We must show a militant spirit, 'must behave like police to ferret out the targets for attack'.

The words of Deng Xiaoping haunted intellectuals in his modern-day attack on Hu Shi. An intensely anticommunist intellectual, Hu wrote his doctoral dissertation on Pragmatic Tendencies in Ancient Chinese Thought and was an enthusiastic advocate of experimentalism and a sometimes critic of the Nationalist government. He was the Nationalist China (Taiwan) ambassador to the United States from 1938 to 1942 and became president of the Academia Sinica in Taiwan. Forums in 1957 followed attacks on Confucius, John Dewey and Hu Shi in the denigration of intellectuals.[29] Hu Shi died in Taiwan in 1962.[30]

Deng said, "For example, I am personally acquainted with all sorts of bad movies, foreign literature, publishing, and music. I was shocked to discover that a certain publishing house is in the process of issuing the Collected Essays of Hu Shi! Why do this? I must firmly oppose it and I am ready to wage a war without mercy! This kind of thing, like the publication of Gone With The Wind or detective stories, shows that the ideological front must establish whether it is Marxism or liberalism that guides us.[31] Just where the hell is China headed? And our socialist culture? The Propaganda department ought to intervene to stop this![32]

One 30-year old intellectual confided "I think Chinese intellectuals should enter leadership. Senior Chinese intellectuals lost everything to our country when they were young, and they were hurt and are very disappointed. This situation forced them to send their children or their students abroad. There were more than 150,000 people (about 110,000 students) who studied in foreign country from 1951 to 1991, but only 50,000 people went back to China. Moreover, most of these 50,000 people went back from Russia before 1958. Naturally some of them did not find living abroad suitable. After suffering long periods of "thought reform", these senior intellectuals never considered changing the situation by themselves. Fortunately, many younger intellectuals are gradually realizing that only they are able to change the recent situation, and that taking part in the Communist Party and leading people to change the situation is their duty.[33]

The Tian An Men incident in Beijing on June 4, 1989, was handled quite differently than in Shanghai were there were no guns fired. The Mayor of Shanghai, a former rightist, didn't want to involve the army. He wanted workers and students to talk reason and that was very effective. According to an older intellectual, "the June 4 incident should not have happened. Young people's patriotism is pure. They certainly didn't have their own agenda. They are the leaders of the next era."[34]

A GENERATION OF VICTIMS

In interviews and letters over the years, Chen Renbing attempted to mention as many persecuted intellectuals as possible so that their stories would not be forgotten. The scope of this work does not allow the inclusion of the majority of cases yet one story serves to illustrate the tragedy of educated elite. Chen described how a prominent physician[35] was arrested as a counter-revolutionary on September 22, 1966. His verdict was suddenly escalated to a death sentence in January 1971. The discussion of his new sentence came to the attention of Premier Zhou Enlai, who thereupon brought it to Mao's attention. Zhou commented that recent foreign opinion voiced alarm when two prominent intellectuals, both United States returned,[36] were executed in Shanghai. According to Chen the rumor circulating in Shanghai was that Zhou said, "We should not permit a third blunder." Zhou decreed that no more killing of top grade intellectuals would be tolerated in Shanghai.

Fortunately, the doctor was granted a reprieve. However, his wife received notice from the Garrison Headquarters on the day of the scheduled shooting, to call for his leftover articles of clothing at four o'clock in the afternoon. Failing that, the family of the prisoner could collect them within 20 days or forfeit said property. Chen said, "Imagine the shock this terse message gave to his wife and two sons."

> Nevertheless, the doctor was not released until January 25, 1979. He was in jail for 12 years and 4 months. Today he is back at his old post, the China Medical Association as senior advisor. The nightmare is over, but, were it not for Premier Zhou's last minute intervention, the doctor would have been another name added to the tragic lists of martyrs and victims.[37]

Merle Goldman in *Literary Dissent in Communist China* explained the party dictum in the early days of the republic that "bright things" be emphasized and elements of backwardness and darkness be de-emphasized.[38] This Pollyanna-style of socialist realism was evident before the Cultural Revolution, when intellectuals offered themselves with all respect to the Party. They abided by every single command the Party gave, particularly during educational reorganization and the thought reform movement. In order to be fit for the demands of our Party it seemed that most intellectuals tried their best to remold themselves.

At the beginning of the Cultural Revolution most intellectuals had absolute trust in the Party. During interviews some intellectuals voiced opinions about their dependence on their Party Committee so that when initial leadership changes were made they felt sorrow and thought somehow the Party had been betrayed because nothing like that had ever happened in the Party's history. The second year after the Cultural Revolution had begun, various corrupt Party practices were exposed and the darkness of the Party revealed itself vividly. At this point intellectuals were awakened yet still found it difficult to criticize each other. Chen Renbing's friend explained:

> It was not until the Cultural Revolution that many secrets about the government were exposed. Then we discovered that the government had demanded too much of us. They cut themselves from the masses. The harder you tried to reshape your thinking, the more severely you would be tortured. Your silence would lead you everywhere.
>
> I said all there was not because there were many stigmas in my former history. I told them about my ideology to seek for help. But they made full use of this opportunity to criticize me. Later I didn't speak out. After some time, many bad deeds done by those cadres, officials were publicized. Everyone of us was totally shocked. It was a shame that such a thing had happened.
>
> In his later years, Mao Zedong was not close to the masses any more. All the demands he made seemed unfeasible. I guess that Mao Zedong wanted to take control. He was afraid that other people might usurp his leadership. Also he was surrounded by the "gang of four." They used him to suppress other people and fight for power. The core of this thinking was wrong. He himself probably at the beginning wanted to fight against the capitalist leaders. He wanted to use this method to cope with other people. It turned out to be terrible.[39]

Many intellectuals shared disdain particularly concerning Mao's politics. For example, when Mao outlined how to deal with different contradictions existing among the people, intellectuals thought that if Mao practiced what he preached it would have worked but considered that perhaps Mao only thought well. Mao was seen as very narrow minded and tended to doubt everyone. What was worse, he did not trust in those who joined the revolution with him. In the *Selected Works of Mao Zedong*, Mao discussed who were friends and who were enemies. Now the situation was dangerous because it appeared that all had become enemies. "Nobody dared to talk to him. So, I think his later years were a great failure."[40]

Chen related that individuals who stood up valiantly against the tyranny were ruthlessly cut down for their defiance. He hoped that these thousands of martyrs taught valuable lessons to those who survived. "If we fail to accept the cardinal lessons, the precious value of human freedom and rights of plain folks to live, think, express oneself, keep personal property and be free, they will have died in vain."[41]

> Democratic rights flagrantly violated by pre-liberation reactionary rule had slowly but surely been restored during the first 17 years of the People's Republic. Sadly, they were demolished overnight during the emergence of Lin Biao and the Gang of Four. Call it anarchy, but the entire judicial and legislative foundation of our nation was usurped by the fascist dictatorship of the Gang. Sun Zhongshan's ideals, preached by Mao Zedong, were thrown overboard, as citizens were killed or compelled to commit suicide. Tortures of middle age vintage were known to have been employed.

> Dawn was late coming, the 10 years dragged on with no relief. At Fudan University, those who survived the first waves of violence and humiliation were either doing labor or living in constant terror of some new wave of abuse.[42]

Citizens were not only deprived of material belongings, bank balances and property rights, they were robbed of their free thought and expression. At the apex of the Cultural Revolution, the most cruel and bestial, animal nature of man emerged.[43] Very tragically, the origins of this immorality was traced to the whims of a great revolutionary leader.[44] In as much as the relationship between Mao and Jiang was business and power, the relationship with his first wife was perceived as wholesome and fruitful. The Chinese people sought out this memory and despised Jiang Qing.

Chen Renbing writes:

> It was really not too hard to trace the storm that evolved into the Cultural Revolution. The Twelfth National Convention of the Chinese Communist Party issued open statements regarding the origins of the Cultural Revolution. The verdicts, in the sight of many, seemed to be fair and just. What happened they decided, came from a Mao's old age stupor, arrogance and over-expanded self-esteem.

Non-Chinese may wonder why Mao adopted an ideology based on the theories of Marx and Lenin since he abhorred the pre-1949 foreign presence in China. One intellectual explained, "I don't think the ideology Mao employed was foreign. What he had been doing, he learned from Chinese history, all those emperors. It's all feudalistic.[45] Perhaps, Mao did not appreciate intellectuals because when he worked at Beijing University in his youth he was looked down upon by the intellectuals. He was nobody there. He was only a clerk in the library[46] and later on he took his revenge.[47]

Mr. Lu Yi commented on the possibility of people's relationships recuperating in the future saying, "That depends on everyone, not just one person. Chen Renbing and I got along as well as brothers. We've eaten much bitterness and all without reason. We really didn't take any bribes, we did not take any money. I don't know how Chinese intellectuals remain cheerful", Mr. Lu explained, "Now the people's standard of living is a little better. But, as for professors, the intellectual's salary is the lowest. Fudan University professors all are quite remarkable. They have given up everything, cultivated and fostered much talent. Mr. Lu exemplifies all the intellectuals who encouraged and contributed to this work by saying, "If you are able to write a book to commemorate Professor Chen Renbing, you will do this not only for him, but for all intellectuals."[48]

Endnotes

1.   According to Ruan Ming's Glossary of Dramatis Personae, "Jiang Qing was Mao's wife and later member of the so-called Gang of Four. Jiang Qing was born in Shandong Province under the name of Li Yunhe. In the 1930s she was a film actress in Shanghai. After divorcing her first husband Jiang Qing traveled to Yan'an in 1938 where she met Mao, and despite reservations of the Central Committee, the chairman married Jiang after he secured a divorce from this third wife. Although Mao initially promised that Jiang Qing would stay out of politics, Jiang became active in 1965 when Yao Wenyuan (late cohort in the 'gang') directed his acid pen at the drama *The Dismissal of Hai Rui from Office* that Yao suggested was a veiled attack on Mao. During the Cultural Revolution, Jiang Qing assumed a prominent role in the Cultural Revolution Small Group led by Chen Boda and in 1967-68 egged on Red Guards to launch vicious assaults on the Party and army. With the purge of Chen Boda and the demise of Lin Biao in 1970-71, Jiang's influence waned; she focused increasingly on foreign policy. In October 1976 she was purged with the other three members of the 'gang' (Zhang Chunqiao, Yao Wenyuan, and Wang Hongwen) and in 1981 was sentenced to death (with a 2-year reprieve) for her role in the Cultural Revolution. Her suicide in prison in 1991 was noted in the Chinese press but ignored on Central China TV. See: Deng Xiaoping Chronicle of an Empire (1992) Westview Pres. P. 257.

2.   Chen Renbing first was targeted by Zhang Chunqiao during the Anti-Rightist Movement. Of one newspaper article appearing about 12 days after Chen Renbing's own article appeared in the newspapers, he said it was from his internal memo, that was conveniently leaked to the newspapers by Zhang Chunqiao. The memo said that he opposed the Party control of film artists, directors and producers. He explained that the ordinary people were not interested in socialist realism,

because it did not depict real life. Naturally, the authorities did not like his point of view.

3.   Interview with Lu Yi 1992

4.   In 1981, the author spent Chinese New Year on northeast Hainan Island. Near " Dragon Horse Commune" was the village of a Fudan University classmate surnamed "Yun". To arrive, we, the first foreign visitors since prior to WW II, had to walk quite a few kilometers in soft sand because there were no roads. In this extremely remote locale was a small ancestral temple whose handmade statuary had been smashed and walls vandalized during the Cultural Revolution. The extent of the damage was shocking given the inaccessibility of the area and small population, all surnamed "Yun" who inhabited the village.

5.   Chen Renbing unpublished biography

6.   Interview with Anonymous May 26, 1992 2:30 PM June 9, 1992

7.   According to Theodore His-en Chen in Thought Reform of the Chinese Intellectuals

8.   Interview with Lu Yi 1992

9.   Interview with Lu Yi 1992

10.   The author lived in China within a few years after the end of the Cultural Revolution and collected about 1,500 unwanted Mao buttons. The pin-on buttons, of varying sizes, are made of plastic, enamel, metal and porcelain. People gladly got rid of them because they feared tossing them in the trash. Of the 1,500, only two are identical. The materials and expenditure necessary to create these buttons is staggering. Paul Fonoroff, longtime friend, has a collection several times larger than the author's.

11.   Interview with Mr. Liu Yi 2:00 P.M. Thursday July 9, 1992 at his home on Wu Kang Road in Shanghai.

12.   Interview with Lu Yi 1992

13.   In a June 20, 1982 interview with Chen Renbing in his Shanghai apartment on Yu De Lu.

14.   82/7/28 interview with Chen Renbing

15.   Chen Renbing unpublished biography

16.   Interview with anonymous 1992, 1993

17.   Chen Renbing unpublished biography

18.   Chen Renbing unpublished biography

19.   Chen Renbing unpublished biography

20.   Lu Yi interview

21.   Interview with Lu Yi

22.   Interview with anonymous

23.   Zhou Enlai, Liu Shaoqi, Zhu De, Dong Biwu, Ye Jianying, Chen Yi, He Long, Nie Rongzhen, Peng Dehuai, Tao Zhu, Hu Yaobang and Ju Choubai

24.   Zheng Zhou et al (1993/7) (*Ling Xiu Yi Zhu: Gong He Guo Xin Sheng Dai Ji Shi*) *Orphans of the Top Leaders: The Actual History of the Republic's Next Generation* by Tuanji Chuban She United Publishing Company p. 365.

25.   Ma Geshun interview 92/6/10 second interview choral conductor

26.   1984 Letter from Chen Renbing to J.F. Ford

27.   Interview with anonymous

28.   Interview with Anonymous May 26, 1992 2:30 PM June 9, 1992

29.   Chen, Theodore His-en in Thought Reform of the Chinese Intellectuals 1960 Hong Kong University Press 5, 15, 114, 126, 129

30.   p 257

31.   Ruan Ming (1992) Deng Xiaoping, Chronicle of an Empire Westview Press: Boulder, CO., p 77

32.   Deng Xiao Ping on Hu Shi Deng Xiaoping: Chronicle of an Empire by Ruan Ming 1992 Boulder CO Westview Press p. 77

33.   Interview with student in pre-departure training program at Shanghai Teacher's University, 9/1993

34.   Interview with Lu Yi

35.   In Germany known as Dr. D.D. Liang

36.   Yin Gongchu and Lu Hungen

37.   Chen Renbing unpublished biography

38.   Merle Goldman in Literary Dissent in Communist China, p. 142

39.   anonymous 1992

40.   anonymous 1992

41.   Chen Renbing unpublished biography

42.   Chen Renbing unpublished biography

43.   Chen pointed out that "Newsweek magazine, February 7, 1983 (page 8) noted 34,000 people died under the Gang of Four's regime. But, I suppose all statistics tend to be guesses. Fudan University sets the number at 41 people who died unnatural deaths from 1966 to 1976."

44.   Chen Renbing unpublished biography

45.   Despite Mao Zedong's enormous power his wife was very much in control. Ye Yonglie relates one anecdote: Mao Zedong's two personal secretaries worked 24-hour shifts, accompanying Mao 7 days a week. Mao asked, "How many persons under my leadership?" One answered, "All the Chinese people are under your leadership." And Mao said "No, only two and a half." My two secretaries and my wife. Jiang Qing will only obey half of my orders.

46.   In the interview, I likened the perception of Mao Zedong by others to that of 'clodhopper. "You mean a 'tu bao zi' (clodhopper)? Yes, a 'tu bao zi'

47.   Interview with Anonymous May 26, 1992 2:30 PM June 9, 1992

48.   Interview with Tao Shaoyuan Shanghai July 1992

Chapter VI: Anticipation

The Enduring Faith and Optimism of Chen Renbing

Before Chen Renbing died in December 1990 he wrote,

> I have never talked much to friends about the plans for my book. Intellectuals in China are always cautious about writing a book, still more about writing an autobiography. Besides VIP's, it is unthinkable that a plain citizen could write a book about himself. The Chinese Constitution does say something about a citizen's right to free speech and publishing. But, one hears of very few, if any, who dare to do the unusual.

> There is no provision anywhere in the laws that one has to send his books for approval. One doesn't know where to send them, either. It happens that very few friends do know that I have written a book in English. I have been careful not to let too many people know the thing until it is printed. For that reason, I would like to advise you to keep the manuscript in your hands for now. It is not improbable that some persons here may have the audacity to order me to surrender the manuscript to them.[1]

Chen wrote his story to show "the efforts of Western friends to help China on the long march of enlightenment and democracy have not been spent in vain." While acknowledging these missionaries, scholars and political figures, Chen Renbing cautioned that the tragedy of 20th century Western-educated Chinese intellectuals[2] must be carefully portrayed. "To this day, I must not be too harsh over the sins of the Cultural Revolution because there is still a die-hard crowd who keep a slave-like worship toward its author."[3]

The fact that Chen failed to yield publications[4] or make an impact in sociology lays at the doorstep of Chinese intellectual's fate.

> When I was working for the Ph.D. in Ann Arbor in 1933-36, I was naturally dreaming that after I went back to China, I would have a lifetime to teach and do research in sociology which was much needed by China. I did teach sociology roughly for 20 years 1936 to 1957. With the exception of 1962-63, I was fired from the professorship for 25 years.[5]

Chen was restored to the teaching staff and his pre-1957 salary was restored in 1981, albeit without retroactive payments. Now in his 70s, Chen revised the manuscripts of a book of readings for the students of world history which contain selections of writings, speeches, documents and histories from the pens of Socrates, Plato, Cicero, Mazzinni, Lincoln, Churchill, Gibbon, Toynbee, Guizot, H.G. Wells, Lin Yutang, John Dewey, Bertrand Russell, Carlyle, Ludwig, Macauley, Roosevelt, Kennedy and Martin Luther King.[6]

> You can see from my selections my deep fondness for the democratic ideals of mankind and the "four freedoms" of Roosevelt. The traditions of democracy have been planted during a century's struggle in the mind of the Chinese people. Dr. Sun Zhongshan fought for them. Other people in China fought for democracy, but failed because of their selfish wanderings. Mao was a tragic case. Since the collapse of the beast-like Cultural Revolution, however, the Chinese people are marching toward new perspectives for Progress, Humanism and Democracy. Otherwise, life will not be worth living here in China.[7]

Chen never lost his faith throughout all the tragedies and found consolation from the words of Paul: "And we know that all things work together for good to them that love God." (Romans 8:28) If there was any good in all these tragic recollections, it was the bitter lesson that one has to pay high prices for freedom and democracy."[8]

Chen always believed he showed unusual honesty and outspoken courage, and, "that justice follows a long and twisted path but truth prevails in the long run."[9] Chen seemed to have confidence that the Chinese Communist Party might be more insightful and perceptive in their criticisms for his own return to legitimacy as the last living of five "unrectified" ("never wrongly branded") rightists.

When Chen died the China Democratic League and Fudan University sponsored a memorial meeting. His family was allowed the special honor of having his ashes interred in the Revolutionary Heroes burial grounds in Shanghai.

Today, there are still some old intellectuals who endured lawlessness and violence and feel more urgently than ever the preciousness of freedom and democracy. Many continue, desperate to lay a groundwork for young people so that what happened won't occur again.

> It took mankind hundreds of years to push barbarism back into history, but it emerged in Nazi Germany and China under the Gang of Four. The only sure guard against the return of that bestial era is true democracy for China, and this is the bitter lesson we have learned. Freedom does not come gratis.[10]

Much of the story of Chen's generation who studied in the United States between 1920 and 1950 has died with those intellectuals. Social issues that sent them overseas to begin with compare with issues the new generation faces as it embarks once again to go abroad and affect change.

Why did intellectuals like Chen Renbing go abroad in order to help China? The chronology of events that shaped the lives of all study in America intellectuals of Chen's generation were traumatic. Feudal mores remained intact throughout withering dynastic demise and chaotic warlord power struggles. Education was heavily influenced by missionaries and western ideology juxtaposed with foreign domination and Japanese invasion.

In 1949, Mao Zedong formed a revolutionary government which enforced nonstop discussion about Thought Reform and Socialist Reeducation and other mass mobilization campaigns When overseas educated exercised what they learned, they got punished for doing what was expected of them as Chinese intellectuals.

This is the story of one man's journey as a spokesman for the Chinese intellectual tradition. Chen Renbing adapted to Mao's regime yet his motives were questioned because he made public his honest interpretation of events. Chen Renbing continued a familiar role carried over from early in his career. He questioned the motives of the government.

His support for the communists in general was overlooked and he paid a tremendous personal price for suspicions that he did not promote the socialist philosophy.

The legacy of Chen Renbing and his contemporaries goes on through the personal influence these individuals passed on to neighbors and friends. Although the overall disposition of Chen's generation of United States returned students was tragic for them as individuals, it can be said that overall the indirect influence is positive and may have paved the way for China's future leaders.

The next generation of intellectuals who have studied abroad are in a position to influence policy in the new millennium and owe a debt of gratitude to their brave predecessors like Chen Renbing.

THE NEW GENERATION

Now, 70 years later, same kind of student exodus repeating the cycle of the 1920s and 1930s. The new generation were born amidst Mao's myopic anti-intellectual campaigns. They coped with famine in the late 1950s, came of age during the Great Proletarian Cultural Revolution when education was disrupted and red guards invaded. They heralded the end of the Cultural Revolution and the downfall of Gang of Four brought the chance to study again.

Today, the new generation faces sweeping economic changes geared more towards capitalism than socialism in the establishment of special economic zones and joint ventures.

China needs to prove to the foreign investor that it should not be treated like other countries experiencing economic difficulty. "It is a bumpy road from socialism to capitalism."[11] China cannot afford to have economic problems due to alignment with communism.

Is China really open to new ideas? Will the 1989 incident at Tian An Men square be repeated and China have to again face global rebuke? Will intellectuals set the stage and do right for children. Will communication remain open or will it once again be shut down? Can intellectuals assert leadership or will their ideas appear too radical? These questions are yet to be answered.

Will these intellectuals eventually endure the same recriminations or will having studied abroad work to China's advantage this time? Intellectuals of Chen's generation repeatedly explained, "what's past is past." They cited the pattern in Chinese history of dynasties falling to peasant revolutionaries. The new movements began fairly but once powerful became corrupt.[12] The question arises, what's going to happen now, because still unknown is how deep changes are toward a more liberal handling of intellectuals.

Recent news reports illustrate how China underscores the ruling Communist Party's renewed determination to keep its fifty year monopoly on political power. In 1998, authorities detained and questioned China Democratic League members and ordered the trial of dissidents for subversion on the charge that they were organizing a would-be opposition party.[13] This crackdown on a sharing of political power is oddly juxtaposed with reports that economic reform has persuaded some of the new generation of Western-educated students to return to China.

> Twenty years ago, senior leader Deng Xiaoping declared that China's best students should pursue advanced degrees in the West. They would become the intellectual propellant for the reforms that launched China from communes and central planning toward markets and laws.

Since then, more than 300,000 Chinese students, many from the nation's top universities have gone abroad to study, usually to the United States. Many have not rushed back to China. Of the 160,000 Chinese students who have gone to the United States, less than 20 percent are estimated to have returned.[14]

Based on the experiences of their predecessors, it is reasonable that many of the first wave of students who went abroad just after the Cultural Revolution opted to remain in the United States.[15] After a few years however, those students who came to the United States to study promptly returned home. They did bring new ideas and technology to once again try to help build China's status in the Pacific rim and global community. Will dispatching intellectuals abroad remain a more forceful way to compete internationally?

Some feel that people who return with advanced degrees are "just the beginning of a reversal of a serious brain drain. Even though their numbers are small, they are becoming an important force for changing China and bringing the outside world closer to home."[16]

China has been influenced by Western ideas and lifestyles through foreign films and magazines and the Internet. One former student revealed that he was "amazed at the changes among my friends when I got back. Political pressure from above is less intense and they are a lot more open to new ideas."[17]

Perhaps, a longitudinal study of the new generation of overseas educated intellectuals will yield insight. In a rudimentary survey conducted in 1992 among 40 scholars attending English classes at Shanghai Teachers College in preparation for their study abroad, three questions were posed:

1.Whom do you wish to model yourself after?
2.What is your career goal?
3.What is your personal goal?

It is beyond the scope of the present study to elaborate on the findings and research concerning the modern group. However, one respondent provides preliminary proof that the intellectual tradition is alive and well in China.

Dr. Zhao Xiaotuan, known as Thomas Zhao M.D., Ph.D. wrote:

I don't wish to model anyone else. I wish and I can do what I want to do My career goal is to do my best for the health of human beings and to contribute myself to probe the secrets of science. My personal goal is to be a good surgeon as well as an outstanding scientist.

Towards a better understanding of the motivation of this group of professionals, a portion of the survey requested they each compose an autobiography. Dr Zhao revealed:

I was born on May 18, 1956, in Nanjng Jiangsu province. My mother has been a lecture. She taught chemistry in a Mechanical Manufacture

School in Wuxi. My father was a Major in People's Liberation Army before 1964 and later become the Dean of school where my mother worked. I have an older brother and two younger sisters. When I was age 3, my grandmother took me to Fujin province in which my mother grew up.

When I was 6 years old, I was sent back to my parents in Wuxi. From 1962 to 1968, I was admitted to elementary school in Wuxi. In that time, I didn't realize how important study is, just as most of the students in this age did. I used every means to play with my friends rather than to study. The comment that my teacher wrote was "fond of playing; the IQ is in the middle level of whole class."

My happy dream was ended in 1969 when the "Great Culture Revolution" involved in whole country. My father was isolated from my family and then the "Red Guards" forced my family to the 'countryside of Huaian in Jiangsu province. In that place, we received the so called "re-education from poor, lower and middle peasants. I had a dark and hard teen-age in countryside, but I got a lot of experience in life and knew how to stand by my own feet. I received my middle school education in Huanshe school for 3 years from 1969 to 1972. In that school, I met several good teachers who did not have high level education but they had much responsibility to teach the students. In that time, I realized the importance of study. I studied so hard that my parents thought something wrong in my mind. I become one of the top 3 best students in a 50-student class.

From 1972 to 1975, I graduated from high school in Liujun. At that time, I was 19 years old. I thought it was time I looked for an job which I would like to do. Being a doctor was my first choice, so I attended a one year "barefoot doctor training course" and worked in a clinic not far from the place my family lived.

In 1978, I attended the first national admission examination after the "Great Cultural Revolution." I was enrolled in Xuzou Medical College. Because I was aware of the chance I have gotten was not easy and the experience of my life encouraged me to study hard and to make my owe future, I got excellent marks in my four year academic studying.

In 1986. I was accepted by Hunan Medical University In Changsha, Hunan province, as a postgraduate student in department of surgery. I dreamed one day I would be a famous surgeon in China. After 3 years of training, I got my medical doctor degree. Then I worked in Zhongshan Hospital, Shanghai Medical University, as a chief resident surgeon. Also in that time I got married and had a boy.

In 1987, I was very lucky to be the last Ph.D. student of Professor Fu Peibin who was one of the most famous surgeons in China. Three years later, I worked in Ruijin hospital of Shanghai Second Medical University as a visiting surgeon. In 1991, I was promoted to assistant clinical professor of general surgery.

From being a medical college student to a clinic-associate professor, in this long time I have given my wife and my son so little time and such poor living conditions that a westerner could not understand or even imagine what a intellectual's living condition will be like in China. Now I arrange to work in the USA as a visiting scholar.[18] I wish I could learn more and make my family life better when I come back.

Overseas educated came back to China with the outlook that they would have decades of contributions ahead of them. Time will tell if this generation of intellectuals will be allowed to have an impact.

Endnotes

1.   Chen Renbing letter to J.F. Ford March 17, 1988
2.   July 7, 1992 letter from sibling to J.F. Ford
3.   Chen Renbing letter to J.F. Ford March 17, 1988
4.   Chen wrote the following books, articles and translations:
   1936—Population Balance (University of Michigan doctoral dissertation)
   1948—Report of a Social Investigation of Shanghai with Special Emphasis on Child Welfare (Chen was co-director of the investigation)
   1949—Toward a Democratic Society (collection of political essays)
   1950—On People's Democracy, a collection of Political essays
   1964—(translation) People's History of Panama
   1983—(re-translation) F. Guizot: History of the English Revolution of 1640
   1986—(compiler) Selected Readings (in English) for Students of World History, Vol. 1 & 2
5.   Chen Renbing letter to Mrs. Sheaff May 18, 1988
6.   Chen explained, "Students in my classes liked this course and the Chinese government has recently ordered to appoint this text for adoption at all history departments in universities an all China. This book will come out in print in 1988."
7.   Chen Renbing letter to Mrs. Sheaff May 18, 1988
8.   Chen Renbing letter to Mrs. Sheaff May 18, 1988
9.   Chen Renbing letter to Mrs. Sheaff May 18, 1988
10.   Chen Renbing letter to Mrs. Sheaff May 18, 1988
11.   Merle Goldman on National Public Radio 10/29/98 commenting on a provincially-owned Chinese company whose debt will have to be bailed out by the central government if they are to stay in business. Professor Goldman said that the central government has reserves of around US$140 billion.
12.   Interview with Lu Yi July 9, 1992
13.   Orlando Sentinel December 17, 1998. "China sets trails for 2 dissidents" The two dissidents are Qin Yongmin and Wang Youcai.

14.   Orlando Sentinel December 15, 1998 "Chinese are drawn back home"
15.   For example some who stayed were part of the sister school exchanges engineered by Yang Chenning between SUNY Stony Brook and Fudan University in Shanghai.
16.   Orlando Sentinel 12/15/98
17.   Orlando Sentinel 12/15/98
18.   Dr. Zhao foreign study plan was to work in the Gastrointestinal division of Cedars-Sinai Medical Center UCLA from September 1 1992 to August 31, 1993. His research project is to study the etiology of human gallbladder gallstones.

Appendix

PERSONS IN CHEN RENBING'S LIFE

Joel Chen (1915-1968) Chen Renbing's younger brother who attended Yale-in-China Medical School and became a surgeon at the Number 7 Military Medical Hospital. Joel was murdered during the Cultural Revolution.

Joses Chen (1912-1974) Chen Renbing's younger brother who graduated with a BA and MA (1933)in Physics from Yenching University and a PhD. in Physics from the University of Southern California in 1950. During the Anti-Rightist Movement he cut off ties with Chen Renbing. Joses was murdered during the Cultural Revolution.

Marcus Chen (1883-1963) Also known as Ch'eng Chonggui, Chen Renbing's father was a evangelical minister of the Swedish American Covenant Church and graduated from Wheaton College.

Martha or Meida Chen (1917-) The elder of Chen Renbing's twin sisters who graduated from Wuhan University with a degree in Chemnistry. Meida worked in Shanghai as a chemical engineer.

Mary or Meiyu Chen (1917-38) The younger of Chen Renbing's twin sisters who was an English major at Wuhan University and died 40 days after graduation.

Mary Chen-nee Li (1882-1974) Chen's mother who was the eldest daughter of a Wuchang herbal doctor.

Chen Yunwei Chen Renbing's second wife. They were married in 1964 and have one son Jiaxin.

Chu Anping Named along with Chen Renbing as a Big Rightist. In June 1980, a determination was announced that Chu was one of the five rightists who was never wrongly capped. Chu graduated from a London university in political science and was the editor and chief of a the Guang Ming Ribao, a newspaper popular among intellectuals.

Feng Yuxiang Northern warlord known as the "Christian General" who appointed Marcus Chen as Chaplain-General to his armies.

John Foster American professor who was colleague of Chen Renbing and Pearl Chen at Central China University.

Hu Shi (1891-1962) Hu graduated from Cornell and Columbia universities and was student and interpreter for his mentor John Dewey. Hu is considered the originator of the Chinese literary renaissance because he created the 'bai wen' colloquial writing style.

Jiang Jiesi (1866-1975) Also known as Chiang Kai-shek, leader of the Nationalist government after the death of Sun Zhongshan, fled the mainland to Taiwan when defeated by Mao Zedong in the Chinese civil war.

Pearl Liu nee Liu Mingjun (1903-1974) Chen Renbing's first wife Pearl graduated from Syracuse University with a MA in Botany and the University of Michigan at Ann Arbor with a PhD. in botany.

Li Wenyi (1902-) Chen Renbing's maternal aunt, leader of the China Democratic League, widow of Lo Yinong Communist martyr of the 1927 Shanghai Worker's Uprising.

Luo Longji (1898-1965) Luo graduated from Qinghua Preparatory College, attended the London School of Economics and Columbia University. At the first China Democratic League organizational meeting 19 March 1941, Luo was elected to the executive committee. After 1949 Luo was a vice-president of the League and Forest Industry Minister. Chen Renbing considered Luo his political mentor. In June 1980, a determination was announced that Luo was one of the five rightists who was never wrongly capped. He died of high blood pressure in 1965.

Lu Yi Well-known Shanghai newspaper editor who came to know Chen Renbing very well during their mutual incarceration during the Anti-Rightist movement.

Mao Zedong (1893-1976) Also known as Mao Tse-tung, revolutionary, philosopher and Chinese Communist leader. Chairman of the People's Republic of China 1949-1959 and chairman of the Communist Party from 1943-1976.

Peng Wenyin Qinghua Preparatory classmate of Luo Longji who graduated from the University of Wisconsin with a MA in political science. Before 1949, Peng was a professor at Shanghai Law College. He died in 1962 before the start of the Cultural Revolution. In June 1980, a determination was announced that Peng was one of the five rightists who was never wrongly capped.

Gordon Poteat (1890-1985) American missionary who along with his wife spent from 1915-1919 in Kaifeng and from 1921-1927 and from 1930-37 on the faculty of the University of Shanghai as a representative of the Northern Baptist Convention. Gordon Poteat and his father Edwin, who was later the president of Furman College, both taught Chen Renbing when he was a student at the University of Shanghai.

Helen Carruthers Poteat (1891-1983) Phi Beta Kappa graduate of Dickenson College served as a missionary alongside her husband and also taught courses at the University of Shanghai. Daughter Ann Poteat was Chen Renbing's classmate.

Sun Zhongshan (18-1925) Also known as Sun Yat-sen, is revered as the Father of Modern China. Sun was a revolutionary, statesman, philosopher who formulated the Three Principles of the People, nationalism, democracy, and people's livelihood.

Zhang Bochun German educated who graduated in 1941. At the first China Democratic League organizational meeting, Zhang was elected executive committee president. Zhang was Ministry of Transportation for ocean going vessels. In June 1980, a determination was announced that Zhang was one of the five rightists who was never wrongly capped.

Zhou Enlai (1898-1976) Also known as Chou Enlai, was second in command to Mao Zedong, Zhou remained popular with the Chinese people until his death and in whose name the protests that ended the Cultural Revolution occurred.

Note on Chinese Glossary

Chinese pinyin romanization is utilized and other well known forms of usage are listed. The Chinese characters are written in the simplified version. In the case of personal names, some prefer complex style characters. For uniformity this glossary uses only one style. Refer to a detailed Chinese dictionary for conversions.

Pinyin Romanization	Other	Character
1. Aiguo Aijiao Liang Quan Qimei		爱国爱教 两全其美
Love Country and Church At The Same Time		
2. Bai Yang		白 杨
3. Baojia Weiguo	Protect Home and Country	保家卫国
4. Bijing Shi Tiaocilu Yeyiduan Jue Shengji		毕竟是条死路 业己断绝生机
A dead end after all All chance of living has ceased		
5. Cao Yu	Tsao Yu	曹禺
6. Chen Chonggui	Chen Chung Kwei	陈崇贵
	Marcus Cheng	
7. Chen Chongfu		陈崇富
8. Cheng Chonghua		陈崇华
9. Chen Chongrong		陈崇荣
10. Chen Chongshou		陈崇寿
11. Chen Duxiu	Chen Tu Hsiu	陈独秀
12. Chen Futing		陈伏亭

Pinyin Romanization	Other	Character
13. Chen Gongzhuo	Joshua Chen	陈公绰
14. Chen Guofu		陈果夫
15. Chen Lifu		陈立夫
16. Chen Meian	Merriam Chen	陈美安
17. Chen Meida	Martha Chen	陈美大
18. Chen Meiyu	Mary Chen	陈美玉
19. Chen Renbing	Chen Jen Ping John Chen	陈仁炳
20. Chen Renhe	Jonah Chen	陈仁和
21. Chen Renlie	Joses Chen	陈仁烈
22. Chen Yunwei	Mrs. Chen Renbing (2)	陈云慰
23. Chen Renteng	Joel Chen	陈仁腾
24. Chen Zonghai	Chen Chunghai	陈宗海
25. Chu Anping	Chu An Ping	储安平
26. Da Chuan Lian	Grand Liason Tour	大串连
27. Dazhang Qigu Zhenya Fangeming Fight Counterrevolutionaries with banners unfurled and drums rumbling		大张旗鼓 镇压大革命
28. Deng Xiaoping	Deng Shao Ping	邓小平

Pinyin Romanization	Other	Character
29. Dong Biwu	Tung Bi Wu	董必武
30. Du Tingxiu	T.S. Tu	杜廷修
31. Fan Youpai Yundong	Anti-Rightists Movement	反右派运动
32. Feng Yuxiang	Feng Yu Hsiang Christian General	冯玉祥
33. Fudan Daxue	Fudan University	復旦大学
34. Guomingdang	Kuomingtang	国民党
35. Hong Wei Bing	Red Guards	红卫兵
36. Hong Xiuquan	Hung Hsiu Chuan	洪秀全
37. Hu Feng		胡风
38. Hu Shi	Hu Shih	胡适
39. Huai Hai Lu	Huaihai Road	淮海路
40. Hui Wen	Peking Academy	惠文
41. Zhangjiakou	Kalgan	张家口
42. Jiang Jieshi	Chiang Kai-shek	蒋介石
43. Jiang Qing	Madame Mao Zedong	江青
44. Jingzhou	Kingchow	荆州
45. *Jin Zhao Ji*	*Todays Collections*	今朝集
46. Jiujiang	Kiukang	九江

Pinyin Romanization	Other	Character
47. Junzhou	Chuinchow	均 州
48. Kagawa Toyohiko		賀川豊彦
49. Kong Xiangxi	H.H. Kung	孔 祥 熙
50. Lan Ji	Flip Flap	兰 集
51. *Lei Yu*	*Thunderstorm*	雷 雨
52. Li Dazhao	Li Ta Chao	李 大 钊
53. Li Gongpu		李 公 朴
54. Li Huiwen	Mary Li Mrs. Marcus Cheng	李 辉 文
55. Li Wenyi	Li Cheshi	李 文 宜
56. Liang Yinbao		梁 音 宝
57. Lin Biao		林 彪
58. Liu Bocheng Yuanshuai	Marshall Liu Bo Cheng	刘伯乘元帅
59. Liu Mingjun	Pearl Liu Mrs. Chen Renbing (1)	刘 明 君
60. Liu Shaoqi		刘少奇
61. Liu Zhanen	Herman C.E. Liu	刘 湛 恩
62. Lu Xun	Lu Hsun	鲁 迅
63. Lu Yi		陆 诒

Pinyin Romanization	Other	Character
64. Luo Longji	Lo Lung Chi	罗隆基
65. Luo Yinong		罗亦农
66. Mao Zedong	Mao Tse Tung	毛泽东
67. Minzhujian Guohui	Democratic Society for National Reconstruction	民主建国会
68. Niugui Sheshen	Oxen Devils Serpent Spirits	牛鬼蛇神
69. Peng Wenying		彭文应
70. Qian Weichang		钱伟长
71. Qiangquan Wu Gongli	No justice out of force	强权无公理
Ruoguo Wu Waiji	No diplomacy for a weak country	弱国无外交
72. Qinghua Daxue	Tsinghua University	清华大学
73. San Fan Yundong	Three Opposition Movement	三反运动
74. San Min Zhuyi	Three Principles of the People	三民主义
75. Si Ren Bang	Gang of Four	四人帮
76. Sixiang Gaizao Yundong	Thought Reform Movement	思想改造
77. Song Ziwen	T.V. Soong	宋子文
78. Sun Yu		孙瑜
79. Sun Zhongshan	Sun Yat Sen	孙中山
80. Tian An Men		天安门

Pinyin Romanization	Other	Character
81. *Tian Feng*	*Tian Feng*	天 凤
82. Taiping Tianguo	Kingdom of Heavenly Peace	太平天国
83. Wang Hongwen		王 洪 文
84. Wang Zaoshi	Wang Chao Shih	王 造 时
85. Wang Zhenting	C.T. Wang	王 正 廷
86. *Wei Yin*	*The Still Voice*	微 音
87. Wenhua Da Geming	Cultural Revolution	文化大革命
88. Wen Yiduo		闻 一 多
89. Wuhan Hechangtuan	Wuhan Songsters	武汉合唱团
90. Wuchang		武 昌
91. Wu Fan Yundong	Five Opposition Movement	五反运动
92. Wu Si Yundong	May Fourth Movement	五四运动
93. Wu Yaozhong	Y.T. Wu	吴 耀 宗
94. Wu Yifang		吴 贻 芳
95. Wu Yin		吴 茵
96. Wu Yonggang		吴 永 刚
97. Xiang Kun	Hsiang Kun	项 堃
98. Xibei Bianfang Duban	Northwest Border Defense	西北边防督办
99. Xiaogan Xian	Shaogan County	孝 感 县

Pinyin Romanization	Other	Character
100. Xin Qing Nian	New Youth	新青年
101. Xiu Cai		秀才
102. Xuan Dao Hui	American Mission Church	宣道会
103. Yang Mou	Open Traps	阳谋
104. Yao Wenyuan		姚文元
105. Yelu	Yale	耶鲁
106. Yin Mou	Hidden Traps	阴谋
107. *Yuanye*	*The Plains*	原野
108. Zao Fan Pai	Rebels at Fudan University	造反派
109. Zhang Chunqiao		张春桥
110. Zhang Yunfa		张云发
111. Zeng Guofang	Tseng Kuo Fang	曾国藩
112. Zong Gan Shi	Chaplain General	总干事
113. Zhonghua Budaocu Jin Hui	Chinese Society for Evangelism	中华布道促进会
114. Zhonghua Mingzhu Zhengtuan Tongmeihui	China Democratic League	中华民主政团同盟会
115. Zhou Enlai	Chou En Lai	周恩来
116. Zhu De	Chu Te	朱德
117. Zou Taofen		邹韬奋

References

Chen Daisun, interviewed by J.F. Ford, 17 May 1982 at Qinghua University, field notes in author's possession.

Chen, Meida and members of the Three Self Patriotic Movement. (1991). *Honoring the memory of Reverend Chen Chonggui*. Shanghai Publishing Company: Shanghai, PRC.
Interviewed by J.F. Ford, 18 June 1992 at her home near Lu Xun Park, Shanghai, transcripts in author's possession.

Chen Renbing, unpublished biography.
Interviews by J.F. Ford 1981 January-May 1982 at his home on Yu De Road, Shanghai.
Letters to J.F. Ford from 1982-1988.
Photos copied by J.F. Ford, all materials in author's possession.

Chen, T. H. (1981). *Chinese education since 1949: Academic and revolutionary models*. New York: Pergamon Press
(1960). *Thought reform of the Chinese intellectuals*. Hong Kong University Press: Hong Kong.

Fairbank, J.K. (1992) China: a new history, Belknap Press of Harvard University Press, Cambridge, MA., p. 53.

Foster, Jane, A. Diary entry February 20, 1981.

Foster, John, B. Diary entry February 19, 1981.
Interviewed by J.F. Ford Spring 1992 and Spring 1993, transcripts in author's possession.
Letter to J.F. Ford 10 October 1992.

Goldman, M. (1967). *Literary dissent in Communist China. Harvard East Asian, Series Number 29*. Cambridge, MA: Harvard University Press.

Greider, J. B. (19). *Hu Shih and the Chinese renaissance: Liberalism in the Chinese revolution 1917-1937.* Cambridge, MA: Harvard University Press.

Guangming Ribao newspaper 7 July 1957.

Hsu, I. (1995). *The Rise of Modern China (2nd ed.).* Oxford University Press: London.

Jeans, R. B. (1992). *Roads not taken: The struggle of opposition parties in the twentieth century.* Boulder, CO: Westview Press.

Keenan, B. (1977). *The Dewey experiment in China: Educational reform and political power in the early republic: Council on East Asain Studies Harvard University.* Cambridge, MA: Harvard University Press.

Liberation Daily newspaper of Shanghai 14,15,27 June 1957 and 14 July 1957.

Li, M. (1990). *Hu Shi and his Deweyan reconstruction of Chinese history.* Unpublished doctoral dissertation, Boston University.

Li Wenyi Letters to J.F. Ford 7 June 1992 and 6 July 1992.

Lu Yi, Interviewed by J.F. Ford at his home on Wu Kang Road, Shanghai 9 July, 1992.Transcripts in author's possession.

New York Times 2,5,16 July 1957.

Poteat, G. (1924). *Home letters from China.* The Sunday School Board of the Southern Baptist Convention, New York.
Stand By For China. Friendship Press, NY.
Interviewed by J.F. Ford 1982-1983 at his home on Arlington Way, Ormond Beach, FL. Transcripts in the possession of the author.

Qinghua Weekly. English language supplement of weekly student newspaper of Qinghua Preparatory College for 1919 and 1920.

Ransom, G. T. (1925). *Science and education in China: A survey of the present status and program for progressive improvement.* Shanghai: The Commercial Press Ltd.

Renmin Ribao, People's Daily newspaper 14,15,26 June 1957 and 14,18 July 1957.

Roberg, T. (1992, February/May). Marcus Ch'eng and the covenant China mission. *The Convenant Quarterly, XLX,* (1-2).

Ruan Ming. (1992) *Deng Xiao Ping: Chronicle of an Empire.* Western Press, Boulder, Co.

Selected Works of Mao Zedong, Vol. V. (1977) Mao Zhu Xi Xuan Ji, Di Wu Juan Peoples Publishing Company, Beijng.

Tan Jiazhen, interviewed by J.F. Ford at Fudan University 1981 and 1982 and 4-15 July 1992 at his home near Huaihai Road in Shanghai.Field notes and transcripts in author's possession.

Tao Shaoyuan, interviewed by J.F. Ford July 1992 at the Foreign Guest House of Shanghai Teacher's College. Transcripts in author's possession.

Tong Shibai, interviewed by J.F. Ford 10 May 1982 at Qinghua University, Beijing. Field notes in author's possession.

Tiao, Shaer, editor. (1993) Zhong Guo Bai Ming Da You Pai *China's 100 Famous Big Rightists*. Xin Hua Publishing Company, Beijing.

Wang, Y.C.(1966) *Chinese Intellectuals and the West 1872-1949*. Pergamon Press, New York.

Wen Hui Bao newspaper 24 June 1957 and 6,7 July 1957, and 6 September 1957.

Weiss, R. F.(1985). *Lu Xun: A Chinese writer for all times*. Beijing, PRC: New World Press.

Ye Yonglie (1992) Chen Zhong De 1957, *Heavy Hearted 1957*.Bai Hua Zhou Wen Yi Publishing Company, Nanchang, PRC.

Zheng Zhou et al. (1993) Ling Xiu Yi Zhu: Gong He Guo Xin Sheng Dai Ji Shi. *Orphans of the Top Leaders: The Actual History of the Republic's Next Generation*. Tuanji Chubanshi (United Publishing Company, Beijing.

Index

For Product Safety Concerns and Information please contact our EU
representative GPSR@taylorandfrancis.com
Taylor & Francis Verlag GmbH, Kaufingerstraße 24, 80331 München, Germany